# Personal Development

## Book 1

Kenneth Rouse

OXFORD

Level 8, 737 Bourke Street, Docklands, Victoria 3008, Australia

Oxford University Press is a department of the University of Oxford. It furthers the University's objective of excellence in research, scholarship, and education by publishing worldwide in

Oxford New York

Auckland Cape Town Dar es Salaam Hong Kong Karachi Kuala Lumpur Madrid Melbourne Mexico City Nairobi New Delhi Shanghai Taipei Toronto

With offices in

Argentina Austria Brazil Chile Czech Republic France Greece Guatemala Hungary Italy Japan Poland Portugal Singapore South Korea Switzerland Thailand Turkey Ukraine Vietnam



First published 2005
Reprinted 2006, 2008, 2009, 2011, 2012, 2013 (third), 2014 (four times), 2016, 2017, 2018, 2022 (twice), 2023, 2025



ISBN 978 0 19 555115 0

Typeset by Lynn Twelftree
Printed in China by Golden Cup Printing Co Ltd

Oxford University Press Australia & New Zealand is committed to sourcing paper responsibly.

**Acknowledgment**
This book was developed with the support of the Australian Government through the Curriculum Reform Implementation Project.

# Contents

# Contents

# Secretary's Message

The Upper Primary Personal Development Syllabus is based on the Curriculum Principles of Our Way of Life and Integral Human Development that focus on healthy living, an active lifestyle, pride in our culture, lifestyles and values, the importance of relationships, and living and working together harmoniously. Students will play an informed role in both individual and community actions that will foster physical, social, emotional, mental and spiritual wellbeing.

This syllabus addresses a wide range of personal, social and community health issues such as reproductive health, growth in population, nutrition, physical activity, safety, HIV and AIDS, drugs and alcohol, the abuse of freedom and rights and peer pressure. Topics of this nature are important issues facing our society today.

Consultation and cooperation between school, home and community will ensure the topics are addressed in a way that supports the role of parents and is sensitive to the values, attitudes, beliefs and practices of the community. All students, both female and male, should be encouraged to participate in all activities to enable them to reach their full potential in all aspects of their lives, and to realise the importance of being a respected, responsible citizen.

Student Books 1 and 2, and the accompanying Teacher Resource Book, have been prepared to provide direct support for the achievement of syllabus outcomes. The content is consistent with, and promotes the teaching and learning models of, the syllabus and the related Department of Education Teachers Guide. These resources encompass a range of material including student activities, advice to teachers, assessment ideas, homework activities, project activities, reference information and a glossary of terms. They are intended to facilitate flexible learning activity for teachers and students, and may be modified and amended to suit local circumstances.

I commend and approve these materials for use in all Upper Primary schools throughout Papua New Guinea

Peter M. Baki

**PETER M BAKI CBE**
Secretary for Education

# 1 Relationships

## Chapter Summary

*In this chapter you will have an opportunity to:*

- ✔ Find out what is meant by a group of people that make up a community
- ✔ Find out about the way that people do things together
- ✔ Describe yourself and the different things that you do
- ✔ Describe the roles that people play in the family and in the community
- ✔ Find out about the behaviour that affects relationships

## Syllabus references

**Strand:** Relationships
**Sub-strand:** Interactions in relationships and groups

**Outcomes:**

6.1.1 Identify groups to which they belong such as family, friends and tribes

6.1.2 Identify different types of relationships and how people interact with each other

6.1.3 Describe themselves through images

6.1.4 Describe changing roles and responsibilities in families as they grow

6.1.5 Demonstrate sharing and cooperative skills

# Interaction in relationships and groups

## WHAT DO WE MEAN BY GROUPS OF PEOPLE?

**Key facts**

- All people and things can be placed into groups depending on various characteristics; this is called grouping or classification.
- Similarities and differences between people and things are used to put them in the same group or in different groups.
- People and things can belong to more than one group.
- People are often identified by other people because they have characteristics that show that they belong to particular groups.
- Our membership of some groups is voluntary but not of other groups; membership of groups can change over time.
- People can be recognised by their achievements within the group – by doing good things or doing things that are difficult.
- People outside a group may not recognise the importance of achievements within a group.

### Groups of people in the community

We all belong to different groups in the community. For example, we are members of a family and may be members of a clan, tribe and village. We may also be members of a church or sporting group.

## THE INFLUENCE OF GROUPS

Groups have an influence on the ways that members of the group behave and the way that they dress. For example, in the New Guinea Islands, both boys and girls often wear a laplap, but in the southern part of the country boys and girls do not often wear a laplap. Families often expect children to behave in a particular way, but this can be different for different families.

*Groups of people at Panakakamwa Island*

| | Everyone | Women | Men | Youth | Boys | Girls |
|---|---|---|---|---|---|---|
| **Church** | Congregation | Cooking group | Choir | Youth group | Sunday School | |
| **Sport** | Spectators | Netball | Soccer | Volleyball | | Netball |
| **School** | Parents and Citizens (P&C) | Teachers | | | Grade or age groups<br>Sports teams | |
| **Other** | Clan or totem groups | | Canoe racing | String band | Marbles | Pacific Island dance group |

*Groups of people in Boroko, Port Moresby*

| | Everyone | Women | Men | Youth | Boys | Girls |
|---|---|---|---|---|---|---|
| **Church (Anglican, United, Catholic)** | Congregation | Mothers' Union | Bible study | Youth group | Sunday school | |
| Sport | Spectators | Touch, soccer, squash | Cricket, rugby, squash | Volleyball | School sports competitions | |
| School | Parents and Citizens (P&C) | Teachers | | | Modified sports | |
| Other | Provincial groups | Business and Professional Women's Association | Apex Club, Rotary Club | Electric band | | |

Another way to look at this is to draw circles that overlap each other. This is a Venn diagram.

Each circle represents membership of a particular group. The biggest circle represents the main group, like a school for example. Smaller circles represent sub-groups within the main group, like classes in a school. Circles that overlap show members of more than one group have *similarities* – perhaps they belong to the same sports team or come from the same village. Circles that do not overlap show that there are *differences* between people in those groups. For some groups, you may be able to *choose* if you are a member or not. For other groups you may not be able to choose – it is decided for you.

So . . . you may be *included* in some groups and *excluded* from other groups.

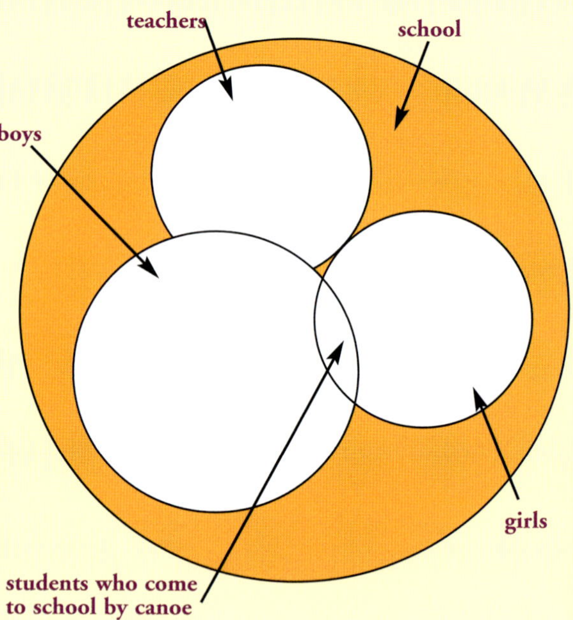


## For you to try

- Draw up a table or Venn diagram like the ones above and write in the names of the groups to which you belong. Remember that there are many different ways to group people – it depends on your point of view. Remember too that some groups overlap with each other.

## For you to try

- List some of the groups to which you belong. Which of these groups do you choose to belong to? Describe a group that you would like to belong to in the future.
- Choose a group to which you belong. In what ways do you behave if you are a positive member of this group?

## Ways that achievements are recognised

When we try to do something that is difficult and we are successful, then we have made an achievement. For example, we might do well in our school work, we might win a sports competition or we might help our family or other people to do something in the community.

Most people like their achievements to be recognised. When other people notice and say something about our achievements we feel good, and this will encourage us to continue to achieve things in our lives.

**Fastest boys**

A team of Grade Six boys from Malolo Community School were the fastest runners in the Sports Competition held over the Queen's Birthday Weekend at Independence Oval. All teams ran well but the Malolo boys just managed to beat their rivals from other schools in the district. The marching competition was won by Bakati Community School. All winners received prizes of sporting equipment donated by local businesses.

**No comps at comp**

This year's Junior Netball competition has been described as the best yet by the organisers. All teams have regularly turned up on time and the decisions of the umpires have been accepted without complaints from players or supporters. All teams have now got their own distinctive uniforms. 'The girls are looking forward to an even better season next year,' the Provincial Sports Coordinator told our reporter.

## DIFFERENT TYPES OF RELATIONSHIPS

People in different cultures live in different ways. There are different kinds of families but everybody has relationships with other people in their family and in the community.

Whether we like it or not, we are related to members of our own family. For example, we must all be a *son* or *daughter* to our *parents*, and we will be a *brother* or *sister* to the other children in our family and a *nephew* or *niece* to our *uncles* and *aunties*. You may be the firstborn in your family with younger brothers and sisters looking up to you. If you are the youngest in the family, you may already be an uncle or an auntie because your elder sister or brother has got married and has started a family.

We also have relationships with people from outside the family. These are our friends, classmates and the people we play with and talk to. We may not be able to choose the members of our own families or even our classmates, but we can choose our friends and playmates. We may choose people to be part of a group because they are good at sport or some other activity, because we get on well together, because they are funny or for other reasons.

### For you to try

- Discuss the ways in which your personal achievements are recognised in different groups in the community. Are t different for different groups?
- In what ways do you think your achievements should be recognised? How do you feel when they are not recogni
- Draw a table similar to the one at the top of page 4 to show the different groups of people in your community.

## For you to try

- List some personal achievements that are recognised, and the way in which they are recognised.
- List some personal achievements that are not recognised and say how you think they should be recognised.

## Some relationships

son
daughter
mother
father
uncle
friend
tambu
aunt
class clown
classmate
best friend
team-mate

# HOW PEOPLE INTERACT WITH EACH OTHER

People who are in a positive relationship with each other do the following things:

- work together
- help each other
- support each another
- show love and concern for each other
- listen to each other

We all need skills in order to be able to have positive relationships with other people and to deal with problems when they occur in relationships. For example, we need to

- be able to tell others how we are feeling
- give our point of view without getting angry or fighting
- learn to sort out problems with other people, such as when they get angry

# CHANGES THAT OCCUR IN RELATIONSHIPS

Many things change in our lives. Some of these may make us happy and others may make us sad. For example:

- babies are born
- people die – sometimes before they are really old
- people get sick
- people may move to live in different places
- people may be in conflict, so that there is trouble in the family or in the community

All of these changes can affect our relationships, so we need to learn to cope with these changes.

## For you to try

- Write a list of your different types of relationships both within your family and outside your family. How does each of these groups help you?

- Choose a sport or some other teamwork activity, like working on a group project. Make a list of the different skills that are needed for the team or group to be successful. You can include the skills that you need in order to be able to work together and the particular skills that are needed for the activity itself. For example, in sport two of the skills might be running fast and throwing a ball accurately. In a project, two of the skills might be having new ideas and finding out information.
- Make a list of the reasons for the changes that occur in relationships.

# Cultural and personal identity

## DIFFERENT WAYS THAT PEOPLE ARE NAMED

Everybody has a name that was given to them when they were born, and which often has a particular meaning. Many Papua New Guineans have a Christian or Western name and a traditional name. Some names are used only in particular parts of Papua New Guinea but not in other parts. Many people also use the name of their father as their family name. Some of you may even have a **nickname** that is given to you by your friends or family because of your position in the family, the way you look or something that you have done in the past. Nicknames can often be funny.

Everybody has particular **characteristics** which make that person different from other people. These characteristics are:

- the place they are from
- the languages they speak
- their appearance, personality and behaviour

## HOW YOU SEE YOURSELF AND HOW OTHERS SEE YOU

We can use these characteristics to describe a person and to understand how they are different from other people. Some of these words may be positive and make us feel good. For example, a person might be described as cooperative, honest and helpful. Other words may be negative and make us feel bad. For example, a person might be described as lazy and rude. Some of these words may be neutral and may not affect the way that we feel.

Our names and characteristics together make up our **identity**.

**Some PNG names**

Kedamwana, Siemanrea, Vali, Kedakwakwa, Koimanrea, Tau, Vagi, Dadavana, Aisi, Pongorea

# For you to try

- Copy and complete the following table.

*My identity table*

| My names<br>Given name(s) | Traditional name(s) | Family name |
|---|---|---|
| | | |
| | | |
| | | |
| **My characteristics**<br>**Ones that make me feel good** | **Ones that make me feel bad** | **Ones that do not affect the way I feel** |
| e.g. careful | e.g. skinny | e.g. boy, girl, highlander, islander |
| | | |
| | | |
| | | |
| | | |
| | | |

- Show your identity table to someone else in your class and tell them about it. Describe how you feel when someone says good things about you. Describe how you feel when someone says things about you that are not true.
- Write a description of yourself and of a friend.

- Write down how you see yourself and how you feel about yourself. Then write down how you think other people see you and what they think of you.

# Changing roles and responsibilities

## ML ROLES AND RESPONSIBILITIES

When people live together in families and communities each person takes on different jobs to help the family and the community. The work is shared or divided, and we say that people have different **roles** and **responsibilities**.

These roles and responsibilities usually depend on your age and gender. For example, parents have to provide food and take care of both children and old people in the family. Old people may no longer be strong enough to work in the garden, but they may cook food and look after the house and take care of children. Children have a lot to learn as they grow up and their responsibility is to love and respect their parents. Older children learn to take more responsibility and help to take care of younger children in many families.

Most people in Papua New Guinea still live in rural villages and many people live close to other members of the same family. So children, parents, grandparents, uncles and aunts may live in the same house or in houses that are close together. This type of family is called an **extended family**. Because people share the different roles and responsibilities, there are many adults to share the work, take care of children and look after old people. The extended family is able to look after members of the family, especially when they need help – when they need to pay school fees, for example, or when people are sick.

## CHANGING ROLES AND RESPONSIBILITIES

Some people are moving away from their home province to live and work in urban areas where they have different roles and responsibilities. Some of these families may be just the parents and the children, and perhaps one or two other relatives to help in the house. This type of family is called a **nuclear family**. In many Western countries people live in nuclear families where there may be only one or two children.

In urban areas one or both parents may be working to earn money to buy the things that the family needs. This means that men may now be helping to look after babies, going to the market, and helping to do the shopping and cooking. At the same time, women may be leaders in the community or working in paid employment.

Gepa's brothers and sisters are the children of all his mothers and fathers

## For you to try

- List the roles and responsibilities of each member of your family or a family that you know well. You could make a table like this:

| Type of family (extended or nuclear) | |
|---|---|
| **Person** | **Roles and responsibilities** |
| Grandmother | |
| Grandfather | |
| Mother | |
| Father | |
| Uncles | |
| Aunts | |
| etc. | |
| Child – eldest | |
| Child – middle | |
| Child – youngest | |

- Choose a different type of family (extended or nuclear) from the one above and again list their roles and responsibilities.

- Draw a family tree similar to the one above, for your family or a family that you know well.

- Identify some traditional roles for men and women and roles that have changed. What are the causes of these changes?

Gepa's cousins are all the children of his aunts and uncles

## OTHER ROLES IN THE COMMUNITY

Communities are made up of individuals who have different roles. In Papua New Guinea many villages have traditional leaders, such as a chief or 'big-man'. When government was first introduced into Papua New Guinea, the patrol officers or **kiaps** chose one of the leaders to be a village constable or **luluai** so that the government had a person who could be a link with the people. When the kiap, **didiman** or another government worker came to the village, they would meet first with the luluai, who would then help to organise the people in the community. For example, at the time of the census they would help the patrol officers to count all the people. Luluais and **tultuls** were given a special cap, laplap and belt as a uniform so that people recognised and respected these men.

Some villages still have traditional leaders, but luluais or tultuls have been replaced with other leaders. For example, there are politicians who are elected to the provincial government and the national government. There may be school teachers and nurses from the local health centre or hospital. There may also be a priest or pastor who takes church services and other church activities. All of these people have different roles and responsibilities.

## For you to try

- Make groups of four or five students who come from the same community. Together make a list of the different roles that people carry out in your community. Each student should choose one of these roles and find out more about it. Each group 'show and tell' with the other students what they have found out.
- Find out about the traditional leaders from your clan or language group. What do they do?

- List some traditional roles for men and women, and some roles that have changed. What are the causes of these changes?

# Managing relationships

All people are different, and one of the most important things that we all have to do is to learn to live *peacefully* together. In order to live peacefully we need to *share* and *cooperate* with each other. We must also *listen* to each other and *understand* each other.

Children in the same family must learn to share with their brothers and sisters, with friends and classmates. Children must learn to cooperate with parents, teachers and other adults. And of course adults need to continue to learn to listen, understand and cooperate with each other in the home, in the community, in church and in the provincial and national government.

We all need to learn healthy ways to cope with problems when we disagree or argue with other people. We need to look for a 'win-win' situation, which means finding an answer to a problem that both or all the people involved think is good for them.

# SOME BEHAVIOUR THAT AFFECTS RELATIONSHIPS 

- Listening or not listening to others
- Sharing or being selfish
- Thinking positively about others or thinking negatively about others
- Looking for a peaceful solution or being angry and violent
- Accepting differences or thinking that you are right

Which of the following ways do you recognise as ways that you and your friends cope with problems involving other people or when you have an argument?

- Fight
- Run away
- Admit that you were wrong
- Tell lies
- Say that you are sorry
- Try to discuss sensibly
- Give in very easily
- Blame somebody else
- Invite someone to take part in something you know they will like
- Keep quiet and refuse to talk
- Ask someone who is not involved to help sort out the problem
- Sulk
- Share food or a drink with the other person
- Pretend to be really angry when you are not
- Break things
- Keep calm and try to think carefully
- Ignore the problem or pretend that nothing is happening
- Tell stories behind the back of the other person

## ML BEING COOPERATIVE

Have you heard about cooperative societies in Papua New Guinea?

**Cooperative societies in Papua New Guinea**

From the 1950s to the 1970s cooperative societies or cooperatives were found in many parts of Papua New Guinea. Cooperatives were businesses owned and controlled by local people according to a set of seven rules agreed by everybody. Members of the cooperative were usually village people who paid money and owned a share in the cooperative. Many cooperatives bought and processed cash crops such as copra and coffee. Many cooperatives also ran trade stores that sold goods to the community at prices that were lower than other businesses. At the end of each year, the profits were shared among the members of the cooperative.

# For you to try

The lists on page 17 may help to do the first two activities, but you will be able to think of other behaviours too:

- Describe some types of behaviour that have a negative effect on relationships.
- Describe some types of behaviour that have a positive effect on relationships.

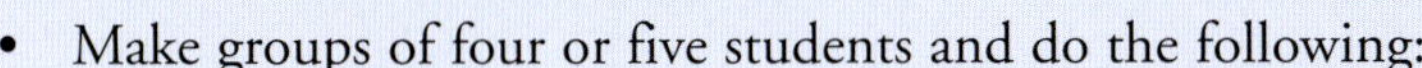

- Make groups of four or five students and do the following:

**New student in class**

Imagine that a new boy or girl has come from another province to join your class half way through the year. The new student has no friends and is feeling very shy and uncomfortable because everything seems different and confusing. List the things that you and your friends will do to help the new student fit in quickly and easily.

If you find this hard to do, imagine that you are the new student. Think what *you* would like people to do to help you settle down quickly.

Show some of the things that you would do to the rest of the class using a little play or drama. One person will play the part of the new student and the others can show what they would do to help the new student.

# Movement and Physical Activity

## Chapter Summary

*In this chapter you will have an opportunity to:*

- ✔ Learn movement skills that are used in games, sports and dance
- ✔ Learn different sequences of movements
- ✔ Find out what it means to be fit and the activities that promote fitness
- ✔ Find out about rules and safety procedures when we play so as to prevent injury
- ✔ Find out more about leisure and recreation
- ✔ Find out about the different roles and responsibilities in games and sport

## Syllabus references

**Strand:** Movement and physical activity
**Sub-strands:** Movement skills, fitness for health, safety, leisure and recreation, roles and responsibilities

**Outcomes:**

6.2.1 Demonstrate movement skills and sequences in a range of physical activities: games, sports and dance

6.2.2 Design movement sequences to allow for differences in ability

6.2.3 Describe what it means to be fit and demonstrate activities that promote health-related fitness

6.2.4 Identify rules and demonstrate safety procedures in play and games

6.2.5 Describe what is meant by leisure and recreation and take part in a variety of relevant leisure and recreational activities

6.2.6 Identify responsibilities attached to different roles in games and sport

## Key facts

- To take part in games, sports and dance we need to learn a range of movement skills.
- When we learn sequences of movements we need to think about the different abilities that people have.
- Being fit means being able to take part in everyday activities without getting tired.
- Exercise and eating the right kind of food help people to be fit.
- Rules and safety procedures in games and sport help to prevent people being injured and make the game fair.
- Leisure and recreation are activities that people do on their own or in groups to have fun and relax, to make new friends, or to develop fitness.
- In some games and in organised sport, there are different roles and responsibilities.

# Movement skills

## MOVEMENT SKILLS USED IN A RANGE OF PHYSICAL ACTIVITIES

When we play games and sports or learn a dance, we need to learn a number of *skills* so that we can take part in the activity. When we begin to learn a new game or dance it can be very frustrating because we are not very good and so we do not enjoy what we are doing. We might feel silly at first, but everyone has to begin to learn new skills at some time. Most of us are not very good at first, but when we *practise regularly* we get better at the activity and so we enjoy it more. When people play sport, it is the person or the team with the best skills that will win the game.

Some of the skills needed in different physical activities are shown below:

| Skill | What do you do? | When is it used? |
|---|---|---|
| **Throwing a ball** | When throwing the ball, look at the ball, look where the ball is going. Throw for<br>speed<br>distance<br>accuracy<br>height<br>This skill needs *hand-eye coordination.*<br> | Just for fun. When playing netball, basketball, softball, cricket, rounders.<br> |
| **Catching a ball** | Keep your eye on the ball, move your body (may need to be quick) so that you are in the right position to reach out and catch the ball without dropping it.<br>This skill also needs *hand-eye coordination.*<br> | Just for fun. When playing netball, basketball, softball, cricket, rounders.<br> |

| Skill | What do you do? | When is it used? |
|---|---|---|
| **Floating and sculling or treading water** | Float on your back or upright in water in which your feet cannot touch the bottom. *Gently* move your arms and legs so that your mouth and nose stay just above the water. With practice you should be able to do this for five minutes or longer.  | Swimming, canoeing and fishing, or just playing in the water. Sculling or treading water makes people confident in the water and is a good survival technique that helps to prevent drowning. Everyone should be able to do this. |
| **Dancing in time to a drum or other musical instrument** | Perform a set of body actions in time with the *rhythm* or music. When dancing in a group you need to coordinate with the other members of the group. | Traditional and modern dancing.  |
| **Coordinate with other members of the team** | Understand the different roles of different players or positions in the team. Carry out your role so that you help the other members of the team. For example, passing the ball and fielding the ball.  | Netball, football, basketball.   |

# For you to try

- Choose a game, sport or dance that is popular in your area. Practise the movement skills that are used in this activity.
- Choose a game or sport that interests you. Identify the skills needed and practise the skills that you can perform.
- Choose one skill from a game or sport that interests you. Explain how this skill will be used to improve your overall performance in the game.

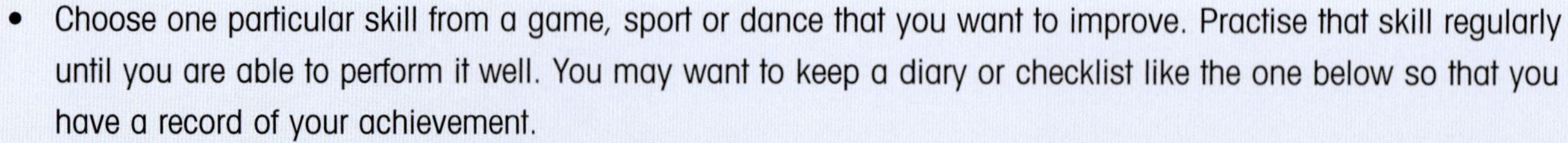

- Choose one particular skill from a game, sport or dance that you want to improve. Practise that skill regularly until you are able to perform it well. You may want to keep a diary or checklist like the one below so that you have a record of your achievement.

| **Name** | | | | |
|---|---|---|---|---|
| **Date** | **Length of jump** | | | |
| | **1.5 m** | **1.6 m** | **1.7 m** | **1.8 m** |
| | | | | |
| | | | | |
| | | | | |

For some activities it is easy to measure an improvement but for others you will need to think about how you will measure your improvement.

# MOVEMENT SEQUENCES FOR DIFFERENT ABILITIES

When we play a sport or perform a dance we usually *combine* a number of different skills in a *sequence* of movements.

For example, when playing basketball, we need to *dribble* the ball between players from the other side and then we need to *pass* the ball on to another player on our side or *shoot* for the goal. When playing volleyball one team *serves* the ball. The team that receives the ball can *touch* the ball only three times before *returning* it over the net in such a way that it is hard for the other team to return it. These are different skills that the players put together in a sequence.

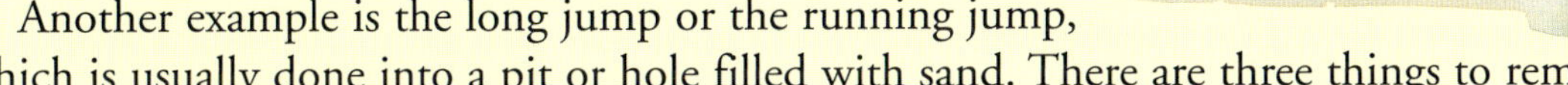

Another example is the long jump or the running jump, which is usually done into a pit or hole filled with sand. There are three things to remember:

1 You must *run fast* towards the take-off point of the long-jump pit.

2 Your *foot must not go over the line.*

3 When you land *you must not fall backwards* or put your hand down behind you because the distance of the jump is measured from the take-off line to the nearest point at which your body hit the sand.

These are three different skills that you need to put together in a sequence to make a good long jump.

## For you to try

- Play a game of tunnel ball in teams.

**Tunnel ball**

1. Each team should have the same number of players (between five and ten).
2. The team stands one behind each other in a line with their legs apart.
3. The person at the front bends forward and carefully throws the ball back between the legs of the team.
4. The person at the back collects the ball and runs to the front and again throws the ball back between the legs of the team.
5. This is repeated until the first person is at the front again.
6. The winning team is the one who finishes first.

Three skills are needed: *throwing* the ball accurately, *picking up* the ball quickly and without dropping it, and *running* quickly. All players use all three skills, but the sequence of skills depends on your position in the line.

Which of the three skills helps a team to win the most?

Try different techniques for throwing the ball between the legs of the team. Which one is best?

As a variation you can have a finish line about ten metres in front of the team so that the last player has to run a little bit further. What difference does this make?

- Set up a number of markers on the ground about two metres apart and a 'goal' with two markers about a metre apart. Practice dribbling a ball between the markers and shooting for the goal. What are the different skills needed?
- Select a combination of basic movement skills from a game or sport and practise the skills.

# Keeping fit

When we say that a person is fit, what does it mean? Test yourself with the following questions:

- Are you able to take part in everyday activities without getting tired?
- Are you able to get your breath back quickly after doing hard physical activity?
- Are you able to relax your mind and your muscles?
- Do you feel happy and energetic?
- Do you get along well with others?

If you can answer 'yes' to these questions, then you are fit. People living in rural areas are often fit because the way that they live means that they take part in a variety of activities. They do a lot of walking or canoe paddling; they may work in the garden and carry water, food and firewood. When we are tired from this sort of work we usually sleep well, and this helps to relax the mind and muscles. People living in the village might not talk about being fit, but they are usually fit because of their activities.

If you answer 'no' to these questions, then you need to take part in more activities that promote fitness, like the ones below. People living in towns may walk little but ride in cars and PMVs, and probably don't work in the garden or have to carry water and firewood. Unless they take part in sport, they may not be involved in much physical activity. Some people also find it hard to relax properly and may not get enough sleep and rest.

# ACTIVITIES THAT PROMOTE FITNESS

| Activity | How does it help? |
|---|---|
| Walking, working in the garden, swimming, running, cycling | Helps heart and lungs; improves muscular strength |
| Stretching | Helps mobility of joints so we can bend our bodies easily |
| Eating the right food, having a good diet, avoiding unhealthy foods | Provides enough energy, protects the body, prevents being overweight and some diseases |
| Getting enough sleep and rest (especially for young people) | Allows the body to repair itself and prepare for the next day |
| Avoiding tobacco, betel nut and too much alcohol | Helps to prevent sickness |

## For you to try

- Make a list of the activities that you and your friends can do in order to keep fit and healthy.
- Imagine that you have a friend or relative who does not understand why it is important to be fit. How would you explain it to them?
- A Carry out a survey to find out what people in your area think about fitness. What do they do in order to be fit? How important do they think it is to keep fit?

# Safety

## ML RULES AND SAFETY PROCEDURES

When we play sport or just play with our friends, it is possible to get hurt. We need a place that is big enough and safe for the activity. If there is something sharp like broken glass, old tins or rusty metal in the area where we play then we can *cut* ourselves, so people playing with bare feet can easily cut their feet. When we play team sports we can *bump* into other people and hurt ourselves, so we have to learn to *dodge* other people. When we are playing a game with a ball we might get hit by the ball, so we have to *watch carefully* all the time.

The most dangerous sports are contact sports like rugby where players have to tackle each other. Players can get *bruised* or might *break a bone*. Sometimes a **sports injury** occurs inside the body where it is not easy to see. Occasionally during a game of rugby, a player might be badly *injured* and later die as a result of the injury. For example, if you have had malaria, you may have an enlarged **spleen** that can be ruptured when you are tackled or fall over. Sports like rugby and boxing can also cause head injuries, which can be dangerous.

All games have *rules* and *safety procedures* that help to make the game safer for the players. Some safety procedures are for the spectators too. For example, if you are watching a game of softball, if there is no net to protect the spectators it is safer to sit behind the batter and the catcher.

# PREVENTING INJURIES

When we are playing games and sport there are a number of things that we can do in order to prevent injuries:

- Remove sharp objects in the area where you are playing
- Follow the rules and safety procedures
- Use the proper equipment for the game – for example, padded gloves to play softball
- Train properly for the sport
- Do not take risks or be silly.

## DEALING WITH SMALL INJURIES

Whenever we play there is always a risk that we will get an injury. Everyone suffers from injuries from time to time and we should know what to do when we get hurt. Most injuries are small and we can treat them ourselves if we have a first aid kit. A first aid kit should contain such things as aspirin, sticking plaster or dressing strips, bandages, disinfectant and antibiotic powder. If the injury is more serious, like a bad cut or a broken leg, then we need to get help from a health worker.

Things to do:

- Have a first aid kit available
- Learn how to treat cuts, scratches, minor burns and bleeding
- Learn when to get help from a parent, teacher or another adult – for example, the health worker at the clinic or health centre

### For you to try

- Choose a game and a place where the game is being played. Write down the rules for playing that game. Write down some safety tips for the players to follow. Include some rules or guidelines about the surroundings.
- Write a story about a group of children who did not follow the rules and safety procedures when playing a game. What happened to them? How did they learn from their experience? Tell your story to the rest of the class, or work in a group to act out your story for the rest of the class.

# Leisure and recreation

When we come to school every day or when we do the same work every day, we often feel tired. We like to do something different in order to relax and enjoy ourselves. For this reason, most people look forward to the weekend and having free time.

The things that we do in order to have a break from our regular activities are known as **leisure** activities or **recreation**. For example, we might sit around and tell stories, sing or listen to music. We might just play with a ball, play some team sport or watch other teams playing in a competition. We might go swimming or fishing. We might go on a picnic to a beach or a river. In some places people take part in canoe races, and in others they have a competition to grow fruit or vegetables, like yams.

## For you to try

- What types of leisure activities do people do in your area? Why do they do these activities? Divide these activities into two groups: activities that have set rules and regulations and those that do not.
- What leisure activities do people do on special days like Independence Anniversary, 16 September?

- How can the leisure facilities and recreational activities be improved in your area? Make some practical suggestions to improve the situation.

## Sporting roles and responsibilities

There are many ways that we play games and sports. We might just play with our friends in order to have fun. You might make two teams to play each other or one class might play against another class. The best players might be chosen to play for the school team and later on you might play in a competition with many teams. For example, some provinces organise a sports carnival for students from different schools in the province. Of course, if you want to win, you will need to train regularly to develop your skills and become really fit.

Players who train hard and have good coaching can end up playing for Papua New Guinea. For example, when we have the South Pacific Games every four years, the best players in each sport play against the best players from the other countries in the region. In some team sports, like rugby league, a few players have been so good that they have played for well-known teams in Australia. In some countries the players can earn money for playing their sport and must train regularly and follow the rules of the club.

When people take part in organised sport or sports competitions, there are many different jobs or roles that people must do in order to make the competition work properly:

- player and team member
- spectator or supporter
- referee
- judge or scorer
- coach
- captain
- manager

Each person involved in a team in a sports competition has his or her own responsibilities and these are different for each role.

## GOOD SPORTING PRACTICES

Everyone involved in a game of sport needs to follow good sporting practices. This includes the players, officials such as the referee, the linesman and score-keeper, and the spectators or supporters. Following good practices will help to make the game fair and enjoyable for everybody and also help to prevent arguments and fights.

| Players | Officials | Spectators or supporters |
|---|---|---|
| Know the rules | Know the rules | Understand the rules |
| Follow the rules | Make good decisions based on the rules | Respect the decisions of the referee — s/he controls the game |
| Respect the decisions of the referee | Be fair and do not favour one side | Be fair |
| Accept that you cannot win every game | Control the game | Understand that the team that wins may not be the one that you support |
| Keep calm even when angry | | Keep calm even when angry |

## For you to try

- Choose a leisure activity that you like to do now or would like to do in the future and list the reasons why you choose this activity.

- Make a poster or prepare a short play to encourage people to take part in leisure or recreation activities because it is good for their health. Display your poster in the classroom, or show your play to other people in your class.

### Senior cop cited

A police inspector was yesterday cited for assaulting a rugby league official during the match between Millennium Brothers and Port Moresby Country Club Royals in Port Moresby.

A referee's report said Inspector Gideon Kauke, who is the vice-president of the Royals RFL Club, and Royals player Mathew Duana assaulted the middle-man who was controlling their game yesterday. Two other players from the Royals camp were also booked for using insulting words.

The incident forced other senior matches to be delayed for about two hours and the main game, between PRK Souths and Eda Ranu Dobo Warriors had to be played under the floodlights.

Brothers thrashed the police team, 26-10.

The club was also cited for a similar incident mid-week in its game against Defence when one of its players allegedly assaulted a linesman.

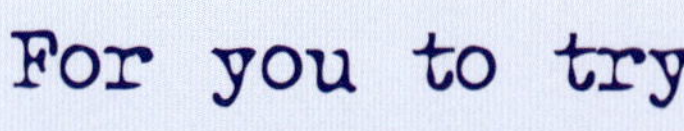


- What would you do to improve the situation described in this newspaper story?

## Responsibilities of team members

- Perform to the best of their ability
- Turn up for practices and games on time
- Attend training
- Follow instructions
- Support other players or performers
- Report things that may cause danger, accidents or other problems

## Responsibilities of a coach

- Help players to develop their skills and fitness
- Encourage fair play
- Discipline players – tell them when they are doing right or wrong
- Ensure a safe environment to prevent injury

## SPORTING GROUPS IN THE COMMUNITY

Games and sports are an important part of life in Papua New Guinea. Many villages have sports competitions, and in towns there are usually more organised sports.

In team sports each member of the team has different roles and responsibilities. For example, in some sports there are players whose job it is to score goals, runs or points. In sports like soccer and rugby the players have to get the ball into the other half of the field and score goals or tries. The role of the players who do this is to **attack**. Other members of the team may be trying to prevent the other side from scoring goals or tries. The role of these players is to **defend**.

Everybody has the responsibility to work together as a team and to try to win. Some team members may have to attack and defend depending on which side has possession of the ball. The team which has good individual players who also support the other members of the team is the one that is most likely to win.

### For you to try

- Choose a physical activity in which you normally take part as a member of a team. List the responsibilities that you carry out and those that you need to improve.
- Choose a physical activity and list the types of roles and responsibilities involved in the activity.
- Choose a physical activity that is not a sport – like preparing a dance. List the responsibilities of the performers and the person who is training the dancers.

Some sports teams have a coach who helps to train the team and teach them the skills needed to play the sport. Sports competitions also need people to help run the competition. The people who run sports competitions may also be players, or may have been players in the past, which gives them an understanding of the sport. Sometimes they are just people who want to help. Some roles of people who run sports competitions are:

- deciding which teams will play each other during each round of the competition. This is also called the **draw**
- keeping careful records of the scores to decide which team has won
- acting as a referee or umpire during each game
- acting as a linesman to decide if the ball has gone out of play
- acting as a timekeeper
- organising a celebration to give prizes to the winners of the competition

# Our Culture, Lifestyle and Values

## Chapter Summary

*In this chapter you will have an opportunity to:*

- ✔ Discuss a number of customs that are important to your culture, such as trading, dancing, initiation, food and clothing, housing
- ✔ Discuss the changes that are taking place in the way that people live and the effect that this is having

## Syllabus references

**Strand**: Our culture, lifestyle and values
**Sub-strands**: Culture and values, lifestyle changes

**Outcomes**:

6.3.1 Describe the customs, rituals and traditions associated with local cultural groups and consider how they influence family and community life

6.3.2 Outline the effects of changes in community lifestyles over a period of time

## Key facts

- Customs, rituals and traditions are still strong in Papua New Guinea.
- There are many differences in the culture of people from different parts of the country.
- We should respect our own culture and that of people from other parts of the country and from other countries.
- Many changes are taking place to the way of life of people in Papua New Guinea and some of these are affecting the culture.

# Culture and values ML

## CULTURES OF LOCAL GROUPS

In Papua New Guinea, the culture of the people is still strong, and there are many differences in the culture of people from different parts of the country. For example, we know that people have been making pottery for thousands of years and people still make clay pots, although the type of pottery varies from place to place. Some other differences are listed below:

- Customs – like bride price
- Beliefs – like believing in spirits such as *puripuri* or *masalai*, sorcery and magic
- Traditions – like making pottery, weaving and carving, making bilums
- Dancing
- Type of food that is grown and the way that it is cooked
- Ceremonies – like the initiation of young people, marriage, funeral ceremonies.

Papua New Guinea is a country that contains many different kinds of people with different languages, cultures and traditions. In many places people are still living a traditional way of life, but there are also many changes taking place.

People who live a traditional way of life can usually get almost all the things that they need from their surroundings. They can grow food in their gardens, go fishing and hunting, make their own clothing and build houses from bush materials. People who live this way of life are sometimes called *subsistence farmers*.

When people have more than they need, they are able to exchange it with other people. For example, when people catch a lot of fish they might give some to other people. Later on, when the people who received the fish make sago, they might give some to the people who caught the fish. This exchange of goods is sometimes called *barter*.

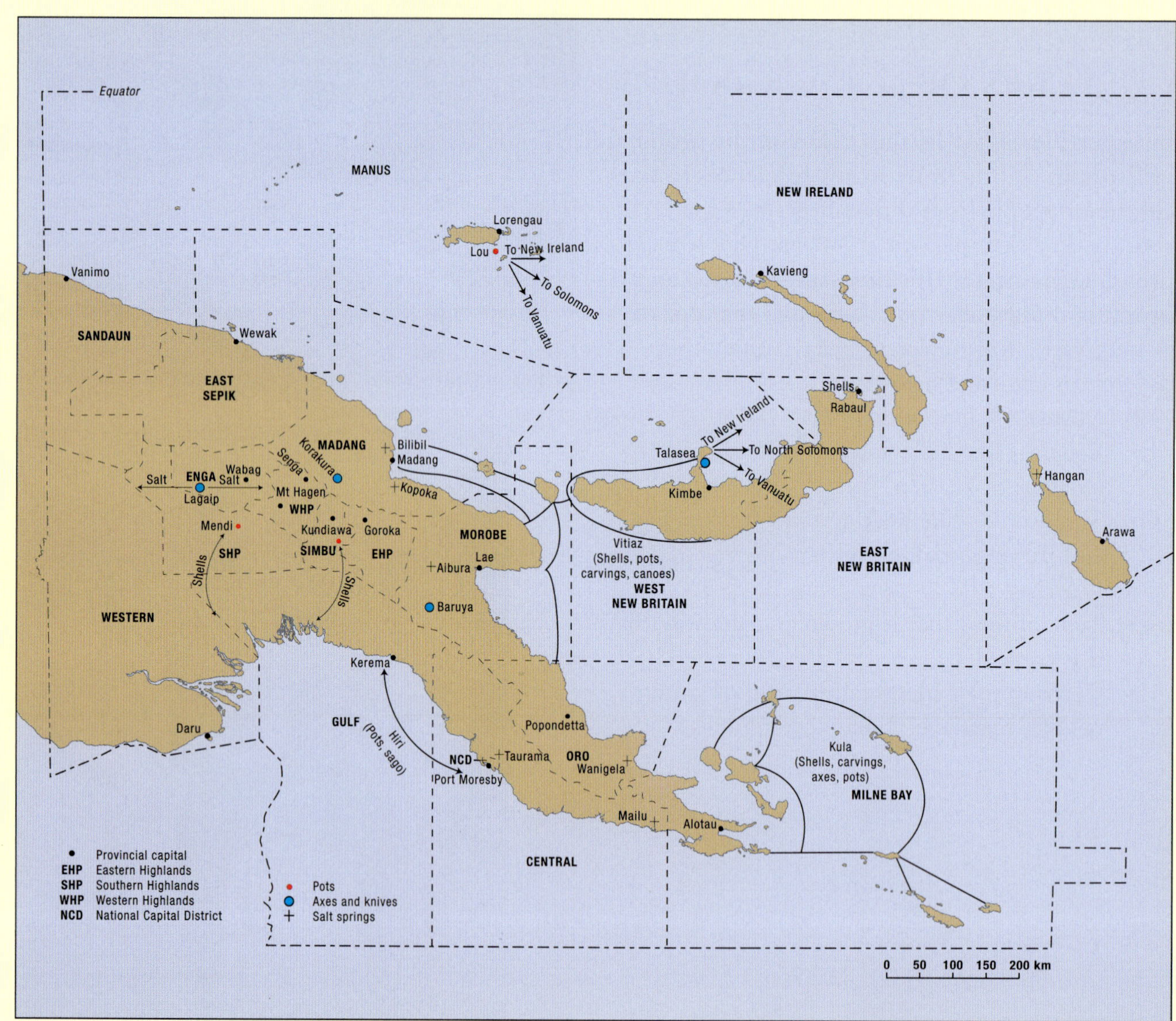


**Map showing Traditional Trade**

One of the earliest ways that people from different parts of Papua New Guinea came to know each other was through *trading*. Trading means exchanging something you have for something that someone else has, and which you want.

In the past trading has been very important to Papua New Guinea. People usually had trading partners and exchanged goods with the same partner every year. Two famous trading voyages were the Hiri in Central Province and the Kula in Milne Bay. In the Hiri, the Motuan people living near Port Moresby travelled in large double canoes called *lakatois*. They exchanged clay pots with the Roro people who live in the Gulf of Papua. In the Kula, people living in the islands of Milne Bay exchanged shell necklaces called *bagi* and armlets with each other. The necklaces moved in one direction around the ring and the armlets moved in the opposite direction.

As Papua New Guinea is developing, people are moving away from their home provinces for schooling, to look for employment and to get married. This means that people from different provinces are now living together in the suburbs of towns and in squatter settlements. In some urban schools there is a mix of students from different provinces. Some people find it difficult to live and work together with people from other provinces but since Papua New Guinea is one nation then everyone must learn how to behave in ways that are acceptable and learn to be tolerant.

## For you to try

- Think about the province you come from or the province where you live. Describe some things from the culture that are special. Why are these things important? How have they influenced your way of living? How are they valued in the community?
- Describe a custom that is important in your area. Include the following: What happens? Who is involved? Why is it important? How has it influenced your way of life? How is it important?

**Girls initiated to women**

People in Wide Bay continue to celebrate the time when girls become young women. "When a girl has her first period then we make a feast to celebrate the fact that she is no longer a child but becoming a woman" our reporter from East New Britain was told. "This is an important and proud occasion for the girl and also tells everybody in the community that she will soon be ready to get married and have children if she wants to. In this way we show the value that we place on girls when they grow up from being a child to being an adult. However, with more young girls attending school, some are having to postpone this ceremony until the end of the school term or the end of the school year," the spokeswoman said.

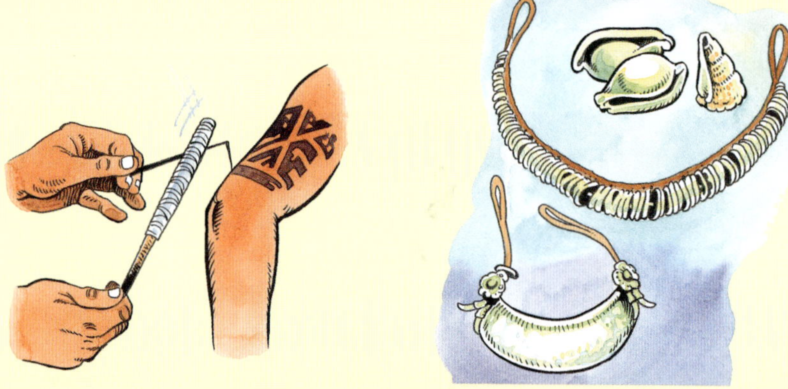

**The value of bride price**

One of the biggest bride price ceremonies ever seen in a Motuan village took place recently. The groom's family gave many shells which were carried by the women on long bamboo poles and also a large sum of money, reported to be tens of thousands of kina. During the ceremony the bride wore a traditional grass skirt on top of her other clothes. Another important part of the ceremony was the preparation and sharing of food, some of which was cooked in clay pots and some of which came from the local supermarket. An old woman told our reporter that when she was young the bride wore only a grass skirt and that all the food was cooked in a traditional way. "Bride price is really about the relationship between families and clans, not just between the bride and groom. Today some people seem to think that it is more like a competition to see who can give the largest amount of money," the woman told our reporter.

**Malanggan ceremony**

Malanggan in New Ireland Province is one of the death ceremonies still being celebrated in PNG, although malanggan also describes the sacred objects that go with the ceremony. The purpose of the ceremony is to remember the person who has died and to mark the initiation into the clan of an adolescent boy who will replace the one who has died. "The ceremony may take many years to prepare, needing extra gardens to be planted and pigs to be bought or raised," a spokesman told our reporter. "The carvings and other objects show people, flowers, fish and crocodiles and mythical creatures in great detail and are brightly painted. Some are carved from tree trunks, like totem poles. Other objects are made from cane, like baskets, and are covered in shells and feathers. The malanggan ceremony unites the people as they do all the hard work and preparation that is needed. During the time leading up to the ceremony, people still feel sad but slowly begin to accept that the person has died," the spokesman said.

## For you to try

- Look at the newspaper story with the heading 'Girls initiated to women.' What is the value of this type of initiation celebration? How is it changing?

- Look at the newspaper story with the heading 'The value of bride price'. What does the heading mean? According to the old woman in the story what is the real meaning of bride price and in what ways has bride price changed? In what ways do you think that bride price will change in the future?
- Look at the newspaper story with the heading 'Malanggan ceremony'. What is the value of this of this custom to the people of New Ireland? In what ways does having several years between the death of the person and the ceremony help the people to cope with the death?

# Ⓐ CULTURAL SYMBOLS

There are many symbols that are important to people who come from a particular culture. For example, if we see someone wearing a bagi necklace made from little red shells, we might guess that the person is from Milne Bay. If we see a girl with pierced ears and red bagi shells in her ear lobes, we might think that she is from the Trobriand Islands. Bagi is an important cultural symbol in Milne Bay Province. For many years bagi has been used in the Kula trading ring and is still important today. Visitors also like to buy and wear bagi when they visit Milne Bay Province.

Some important cultural symbols:

- Necklaces – dog's teeth, Job's tears or strips of bamboo
- Shells like kina and toea, bagi and tabu (shell money)
- Feathers such as Bird of Paradise plumes
- Bilums – especially the size, shape and colours used
- Tattoos on the face and other parts of the body
- Style of dressing
- Food
- Language

## For you to try

- Using ideas from the list above, copy and complete the following table. One example has been done for you.

| **Cultural symbol and where it is from** | **What is it made of? How is it made?** | **Where is it seen? How is it used?** | **Why is it important? What is its purpose?** |
|---|---|---|---|
| Bagi from Milne Bay Province | Little red shells – can be strung together in different lengths | Worn as a necklace or earrings; used in traditional trading | Important in trading relationships. Symbol of wealth. Attractive to look at. |
| | | | |
| | | | |
| | | | |

If your parents come from different provinces or if you are not living in your own province then you can include cultural symbols from both parents and both provinces.

# CHANGES IN CUSTOMS AND TRADITION

Papua New Guinea is a country that is changing very rapidly. There are changes in the way that people dress, and in the food that they grow and eat. In the rural areas people may still grow the same crops they have had for a long time, but new crops have also been introduced. There are also new ways of taking care of crops such as using chemical fertilisers to make them grow better and chemicals to kill insect pests. Traditional singing and dancing are still important, but many people now also like to listen to the music from other countries and to dance to popular music.

Some of these changes may be positive and some may be negative. For example, in the past most people ate a healthy traditional diet. Today many people enjoy eating a greater variety of food, but these new foods may not be as healthy as traditional food. Dark green leafy vegetables like aibika are better than English cabbage. Many people like to eat white rice and white bread, but brown rice and brown bread made from wholemeal flour are better foods. And many of the 'fast foods' that people like to eat in towns, like fried chicken and chips, contain too much fat, too much sugar or too much salt. Eating these foods regularly can make people overweight and unhealthy. This problem has been happening in countries like Australia for many years and is beginning to happen in some towns and villages in Papua New Guinea.

## For you to try

- Make groups of four or five students. Discuss the changes in customs and traditions that have taken place in your community. Make a list of these changes and say whether you think each change is positive or negative.

## For you to try

- Think about dressing, food, transport and language. From one of these topics choose a cultural practice, a skill or a belief that we want to keep. Describe what we can do to make sure that we do not lose that practice, skill or belief. Share your ideas with other members of your class.

For example, thinking about food, one way to keep the value of local foods would be to have one day each week when we only eat local foods cooked in a traditional way. Another way would be to serve only traditional food when we serve food to visitors.

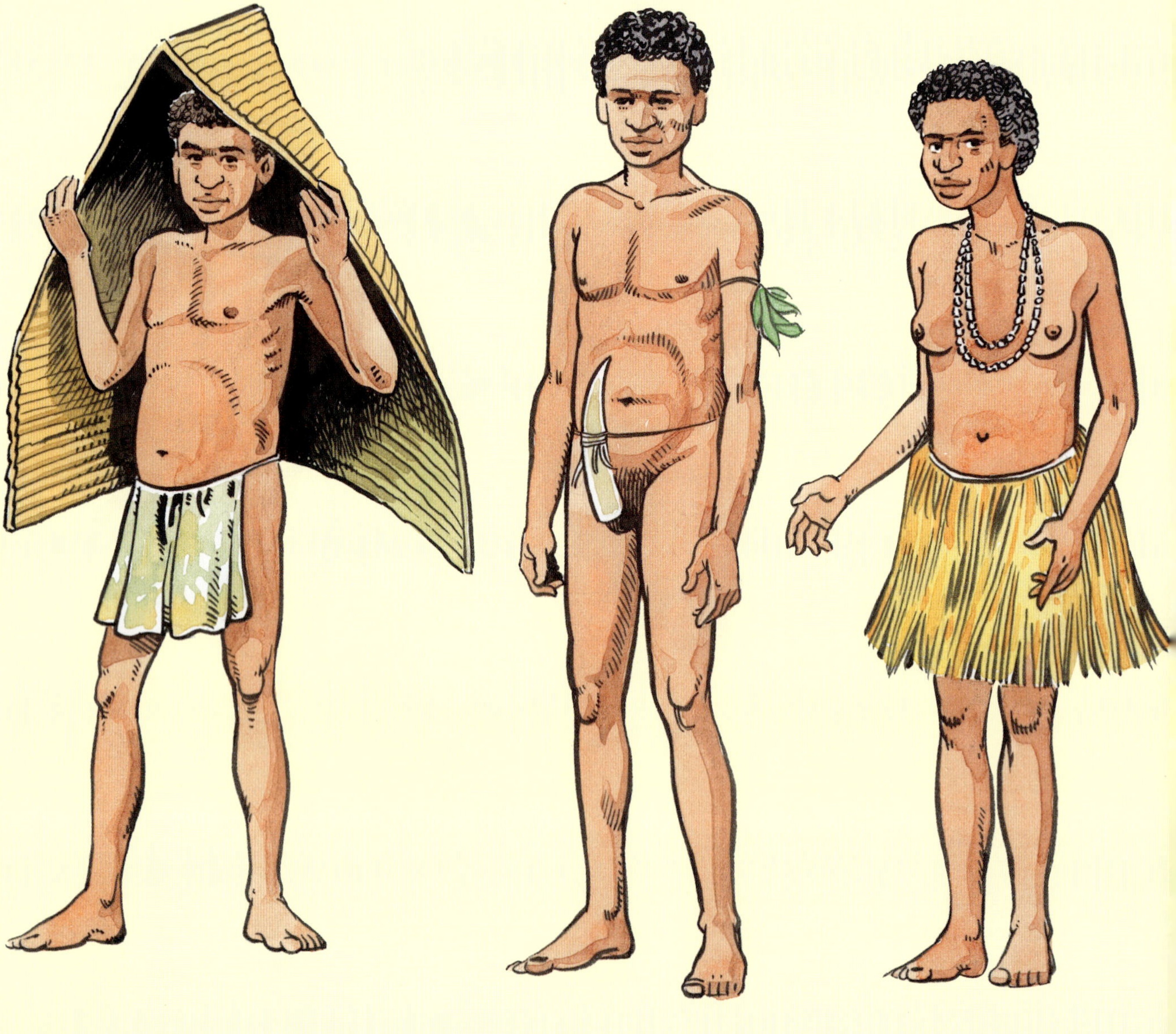

# Lifestyle and changes

Many changes have taken place in the way that people live. Instead of wearing traditional clothes every day, most people now wear modern clothes. Grass skirts, tapa cloth and leaves have been replaced with cotton and polyester. People can make their own traditional clothes, but clothes bought in the store cost money and so people must have cash in order to be able to buy clothes for the family. Traditional clothes can be thrown away when they become old and dirty, but modern clothes need to be washed regularly so we need to buy washing powder.

We need to learn to wear clothes that are suitable for different occasions. When we come to school or play in a sports team, we often wear a uniform so that people know which school or team we belong to. When we go to work in the garden, we know that we are going to get dirty so we don't wear our smart clothes. When we take part in traditional dancing, we should wear our traditional dress with pride to show that we respect our culture.

**Moale goes to town**

Moale had enjoyed her trip to town with her auntie. She had seen a really nice dress in one of the Chinese trade stores and was wondering how she might find enough money to buy it. It would look really good when she went to a party – especially if there was disco dancing.

On the PMV home, her mind started going over something that had happened at school. Her teacher had told them that each group of students had to put on a traditional dance. She had learned some traditional dances from her mother and aunties when she was small, but now that she was getting bigger she felt uncomfortable about wearing a grass skirt, putting feathers in her hair and having her face and body painted. She felt shy, that everybody was looking at her and was wondering how she could avoid having to take part.

When she got home her auntie could see that she was worried about something, and Moale began to tell her why she did not want to take part in the traditional dancing.

Her auntie listened carefully. Then she began to explain that women in their clan were very important and that traditional dance had been passed from the older women to young girls for many generations. She talked about being proud of their culture and about the skill in making grass skirts, and how one day Moale might want to teach her own daughter how to make grass skirts and how to dance.

As her auntie spoke, Moale could see that she was really part of a long line of girls and women from her clan and began to feel a bit better about what her teacher had asked them to do. 'Of course, we won't wear our grass skirts when we go to town,' her auntie said, 'but next time maybe we will be able to buy that nice dress I saw you looking at in the Chinese trade store.'

## For you to try

- Why did Moale feel uncomfortable about taking part in the traditional dancing? Describe some different types of occasion and the style of dress that it is appropriate to wear on those occasions.
- How did Moale's auntie help Moale to feel better about taking part in traditional dancing?

- Carry out a survey to find out about changes that have occurred in your community and people's opinion about these changes. The following table may help you (one example has been filled in already):

| Topic | Changes that have occurred | People's opinion about this change |
| --- | --- | --- |
| Ways of living | | |
| Dress | | |
| Types of food | Bigger choice of food than before, especially food from the store | I like to eat different types of food but they are expensive and small children are asking for many things |
| Trade | | |
| Spiritual beliefs | | |
| Physical changes (buildings, roads) | | |
| Languages | | |

# Health of Individuals and Population

## Chapter Summary

*In this chapter you will have an opportunity to:*

- ✔ Find out about the stages in growth and development that we pass through and our health needs at different stages
- ✔ Find out what makes us like we are
- ✔ Find out different ways to get information about growing up
- ✔ Find out why eating healthy food is important
- ✔ Learn how to prepare a healthy meal
- ✔ Learn how to stay clean and healthy
- ✔ Find out how illnesses are spread and how to protect yourself
- ✔ Learn about dangers at school and at home
- ✔ Find out how people in the community can stay healthy
- ✔ Find out about health services in the community
- ✔ Learn about the use of drugs that help people stay healthy
- ✔ Learn about drugs that can cause problems

## Syllabus references

**Strand:** Health of individuals and population
**Sub-strands:** Growth and development, nutrition, personal health and safety, community health, use of drugs

**Outcomes**

6.4.1 Describe the stages in growth and development and the health needs at various stages

6.4.2 Explore influences of inherited characteristics and environmental factors on growth and development

6.4.3 Investigate various sources of information about sexual development

6.4.4 Explain how choosing and eating healthy food promotes health

6.4.5 Plan and prepare a meal using safe and hygienic methods of food preparation

6.4.6 Describe personal hygiene practices and how they promote personal health

6.4.7 Investigate how illnesses are spread and how they can protect themselves from illness and disease

6.4.8 Identify potentially hazardous situations at school, home and the community

6.4.9 Describe ways in which the community promotes the health of community and individuals

6.4.10 Identify the health services available to various groups in the community

6.4.11 Describe the beneficial and harmful effects of drugs on health

6.4.12 Identify reasons people use drugs

## Key facts

- We all pass through key stages in our **development**: from birth, through infancy and childhood, into puberty and adolescence, then into adulthood and old age, and finally death.
- We all get characteristics from our parents but we are also affected by our surroundings as we grow up.
- Eating healthy food and a balanced diet, taking regular exercise and getting enough rest will help us to grow properly and stay healthy.
- Washing ourselves and our clothes, sheets and towels regularly, and keeping our surroundings clean, also helps us to stay healthy.
- Illnesses can be spread by germs and we can prevent sickness by keeping clean, having vaccinations or immunisations and getting treatment when we are sick.
- There are dangers at school and at home and we need to learn how to avoid these and stay safe.
- Drugs or medicines can help to prevent sickness and can be used to treat people who are sick.
- Some drugs like betel nut, tobacco and alcohol can make people sick.

# Growth and development

## STAGES OF GROWTH AND DEVELOPMENT

Some of the most interesting things that happen to us are the stages that we go through as we grow from a baby into a child and then into an adult.

In their first year of life babies are helpless and need a lot of care from their mothers and fathers. Young babies are called **infants** and this period of time is called *infancy*.

The stage when children change into adults is called **puberty**. The age when this happens varies from person to person but is usually between the ages of ten and seventeen. Girls usually reach puberty about two years earlier than boys. The changes that take place are slow and usually take several years to complete.

### For you to try

- Find out about the different stages in the development of a child (you could choose yourself). At about what age does a child first smile, crawl, walk, run, talk, read, write etc.? What other stages are important?
- Draw a timeline to show childhood or adolescence. On the timeline show the most important changes and the age at which this change occurs.

At puberty girls start to have **periods** and boys start to produce **semen** that contains **sperm**, so it is possible for you to reproduce or to have children. The time between puberty and full adult maturity is called **adolescence**. During adolescence you learn to think and behave as an adult. Adolescence can last for ten years or more and can be a difficult time for some young people, their parents and teachers. During this time some young people find that their feelings are mixed up and their moods change quickly.

We can show these different stages on a time line:

# AREAS OF DEVELOPMENT

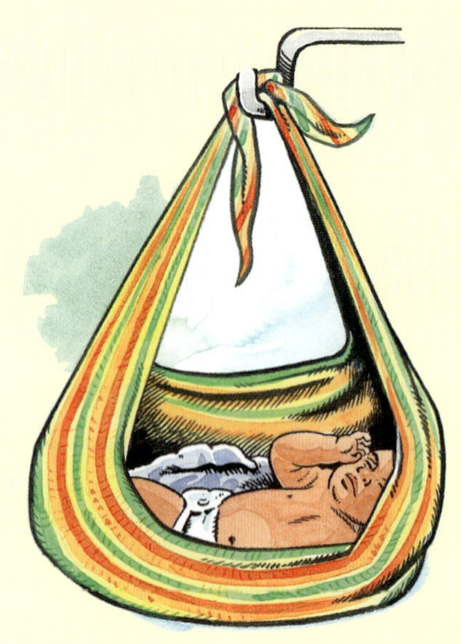

We grow and *develop* in different ways. As we grow up our bodies change in *appearance*. Our bodies change in size and shape. For example, we grow taller and stronger. Babies and children should steadily get *taller* and *heavier*. Nurses weigh babies regularly at the clinic and record their weight in a book to make sure that they are staying healthy. During puberty girls start to develop breasts and boys start to grow beards. Hair also begins to grow under the armpits and in the pubic area. This kind of development is known as *physical development*.

As we grow and develop we learn to think properly, to carry out more difficult tasks and to understand more difficult ideas. For example, most children cannot read, write or do Maths when they come to school, but they can do these things by the time they leave school. This is known as *intellectual development*.

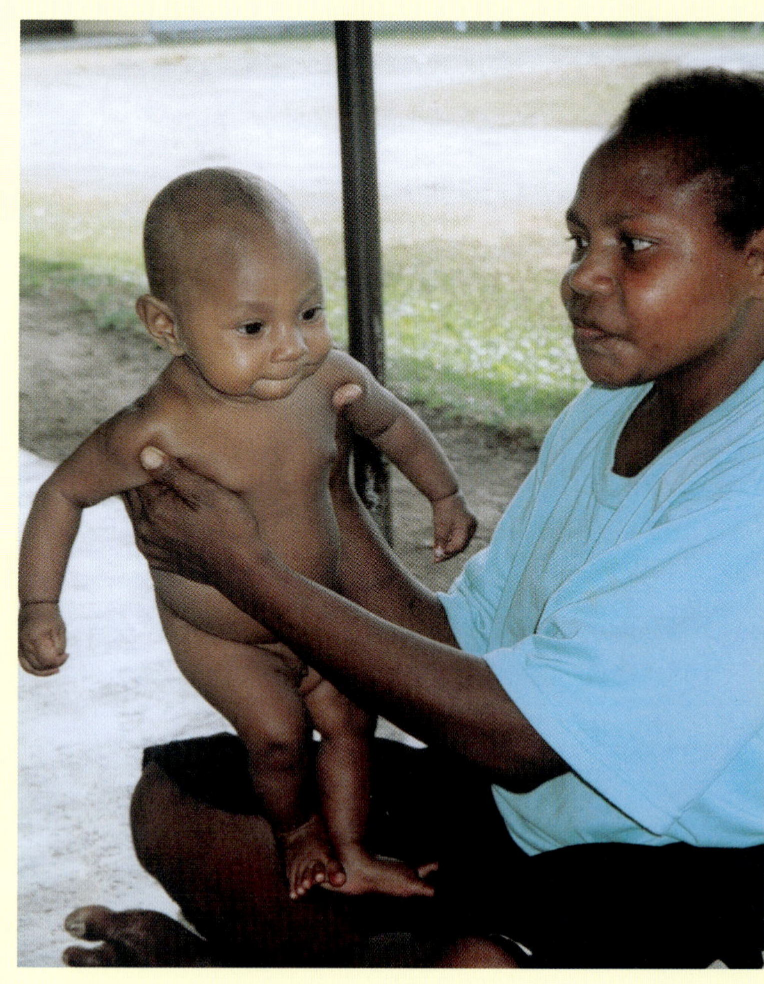

People live together in families and communities, so another change that takes place is in the way that we learn to live with other people. We learn to talk to other people and to share things with them. We also learn to sort out problems with other people. We learn to be independent of our parents by making friendships and cooperating with others. This kind of development is called *social development*.

Babies often cry when they are hungry or thirsty or feeling uncomfortable. Some children also cry when they want something. Some children may get very cross if they do not get what they want immediately. However, as we grow up we learn about other ways to express our feelings or *emotions*. We learn to think about the needs of other people, not just about our own needs. This kind of development is called *emotional development*.

## For you to try

- Interview an adult that you know well. Ask the person about the personal changes that have occurred in his or her life. What responsibilities has the person experienced? List the changes that have occurred in that person's way of life.

## THINGS THAT HELP US GROW AND DEVELOP

- Exercise – walking to school, playing games, swimming, working in the garden.
- Diet – eating different kinds of healthy food like fresh fruit and vegetables; avoiding unhealthy foods that contain too much fat, sugar or salt.
- Rest and sleep – when you are growing, playing sport and studying at school you need lots of rest and sleep.
- Safety – feeling safe and secure at home and in the community helps us to grow and develop well.
- Staying healthy – when children get sick often, it can slow down growth and development.

## For you to try

- Make a set of rules or guidelines to follow in order to care for the body. Explain why each of these rules is important. Discuss what will happen if we do not follow these rules.

# WHAT MAKES US LIKE WE ARE?

Everybody comes from a mother and a father and we usually look like our parents, although there will be some differences as well. For example, if your mother and father both come from the same province then you will also look like someone who comes from that province. If both your parents have dark skin, then it is most likely that you will have dark skin.

Characteristics we get from our parents are:

- colour of skin
- type of hair
- height
- shape of body
- facial features like the size and shape of nose

Because these characteristics are **inherited** from our parents, there is really nothing that we can do to change them. As we grow up we learn to accept the things that we cannot change.

We also know that there are things that we can change that will affect our bodies. For example, we know that eating good food, taking regular exercise and having enough rest all help children to grow well. A child with tall parents will not grow tall without eating good food and getting enough sleep.

Many of these things that we can change or control come from our surroundings or from the **environment**. Some of these things from our surroundings may change us in positive ways and some may change us in negative ways. For example, if we always sleep in a house that is very smoky, we get lung diseases.

Another example of the way that the environment can affect our bodies is the place where you live. When you live on the coast and then visit the highlands to play sport, you may find that you cannot run as fast as people who live in the highlands. This is because there is less oxygen in the air in the highlands. When you live in the highlands your blood learns to carry more oxygen, so you can run faster without getting tired.

Things in our surroundings or behaviour that can change the way we grow and develop:

- food – type and amount
- exercise that we take
- rest
- feeling safe, not being scared or bullied
- personal habits like smoking and drinking
- keeping clean and hygienic – both your body and the surroundings
- insects like mosquitoes that carry malaria
- pollution – breathing dirty or smoky air, drinking or washing in dirty water
- peer pressure – doing things because your friends do them, or because they 'force' you to do them

Some of these can have a positive effect or a negative effect on the way that we grow and develop. For example, we all need enough food to grow and develop, but if we eat too much we will become overweight, which is not healthy.

## For you to try

- Make groups of three or four students. Choose one of the items from the list above. Discuss how this item can have a negative effect on your growth and development. Make a list of the things that you can do so that this does not stop you growing and developing well. Share your ideas with other groups.

# GROWING UP

When a baby is born the first question people ask is usually 'Is it a boy or a girl?' In other words, people are interested in the **sex** of the baby. The sex that we are continues to be important throughout childhood, adolescence and adulthood.

Boys and girls have different bodies, and as they grow up they become interested in different things. Young boys and girls may play together, but as they get older boys often start to do more things with other boys and often learn a lot from their fathers and uncles. Girls often start to play more with other girls and learn things from their mothers and aunties that are not interesting to boys.

When you are growing up your body changes and you start to have different feelings. Boys and girls become more interested in each other. You often want to know the answers to many questions but may feel shy about asking such questions. Parents and other adults also find it difficult to talk about this topic. However, in order to be healthy we need to understand about our bodies and the way that we think and feel.

**Gender** is the way in which we learn from the community to become girls and boys, men and women. We need to understand what it means to be a boy and what it means to be a girl. We need to understand what it means to be a man and what it means to be a woman. When we understand ourselves and each other, we can learn to have healthy relationships.

**What do we mean by . . .?**

**sex** – being a male or a female. Also means sexual contact between a man and a woman.

**sexuality** – the way that we think, feel and behave because we are a male or a female.

**sexual development** – the changes that take place in our bodies as we develop from a girl to a woman and a boy into a man. The period of sexual development is called *puberty*.

# For you to try

- Copy and complete the following table:

| Places that you get information about sexual development | Is this a good source of information? Why or why not? |
|---|---|
| Newspapers, magazines, radio, television, video | |
| Parents and elders | |
| Teachers | |
| Books | |
| Friends and peers | |

Discuss your ideas with your teacher.

- Write down a question about sexual development on a piece of paper. Do not put your name on the paper. Put the piece of paper in a box. Later on your teacher will go through the questions and sort them out. Your teacher will read out the questions and talk about the answers with the class.

# Nutrition

## EATING HEALTHY FOOD

Food is important to everyone and most people enjoy eating. We need food to stay alive, but food is also important in other ways.

Food can be divided into different groups. *Energy foods* are high in **carbohydrates**. *Body-building foods* are high in **protein**. *Protective foods* are high in vitamins and minerals.

If we do not eat enough food, we feel hungry and eventually we will get sick. If we eat too much of some types of food, we may become overweight or get other types of sickness. It is important to eat enough of the right kind of food every day. This is called eating a *balanced diet*.

When our family eats together we talk about what has happened during the day and enjoy each other's company

During important occasions the food that we prepare and share helps to make the occasion special – like a mumu, for example

**Green, yellow, white – that's right**

The way that a balanced diet is made up of food from the three food groups is shown in the pyramid below.

Fruits and vegetables also have different colours, so another way of eating a balanced diet is to eat different coloured foods. Each day you should try to eat a mixture of red, yellow, green and white foods. Green leaves are very important. Dark green leaves such as aibika or other *kumu* are better than light green leaves.

The way that a food is cooked or prepared is also important. For example, food that is fried contains more fat, and some foods contain extra sugar. Eating food that is high in fat and sugar is not healthy and we should only eat these foods occasionally.

## For you to try

- Carry out a survey to find out what foods you and your friends like best. Make a list like the one below. To count the number of people, use one short vertical line for each person up to four and for the fifth person put a horizontal line through the four lines. Your results will look a bit like a graph and you will easily be able to see which foods are most popular.

| Food | How much do you like this food? | | |
|---|---|---|---|
| | **Really like it** | **Neither like or dislike** | **Do not like it** |
| Sweet potato | | | |
| Aibika | | | |
| Banana | | | |
| Chicken | | | |
| Fish | | | |
| White rice | | | |
| Bread | | | |
| Other | | | |
| | | | |
| | | | |

Show your results to the rest of the class and discuss them. What foods are popular with your classmates? What are the reasons for this?

## For you to try

Use the table below and the pyramid on page 62 to list the foods and drinks that you have consumed in the last three days. Show what each food and drink contains. Two examples have been done for you.

| Food/drink | Energy food | Body-building food (protein) | Protective food |
|---|---|---|---|
| banana | | | |
| lolly water | | | |
| | | | |
| | | | |
| | | | |
| | | | |

Have you eaten a balanced diet in the last three days?

What are the reasons for your choice of foods over the last few days?

How can your diet be improved?

- List five common foods in your area. List five things you could do to improve your nutrition.

# PLANNING AND PREPARING MEALS ML

When we prepare a meal for people to eat, we want the food to be healthy. Healthy food is **nourishing** or *nutritious*. Meals that contain food from the three food groups are nutritious, but too much sugar or fat is not healthy.

We also want the food to taste good and to be safe. Food that is nutritious and tastes good may not be safe to eat if it has not been prepared and stored properly. It is important to learn how to *prepare* and *store* food properly. The way that we prepare and store food is called *food handling.*

### Things to decide when planning and preparing a meal

What type of food will you prepare and cook?
Amount of food – how many people are going to eat?
Quality of the food – is it fresh? Does it look fresh? Does it smell fresh?
Method of food preparation – is it safe and hygienic?
Keep hands, utensils and surfaces clean.
Keep food covered.

### Things needed for food preparation

Kerosene, firewood or gas
Matches, leaves or other wrappers
Cooking utensils
Cleaning materials

### Buying things in the store

What is the best value for money – the cost in relation to the weight or size?
Check expiry date – not out of date

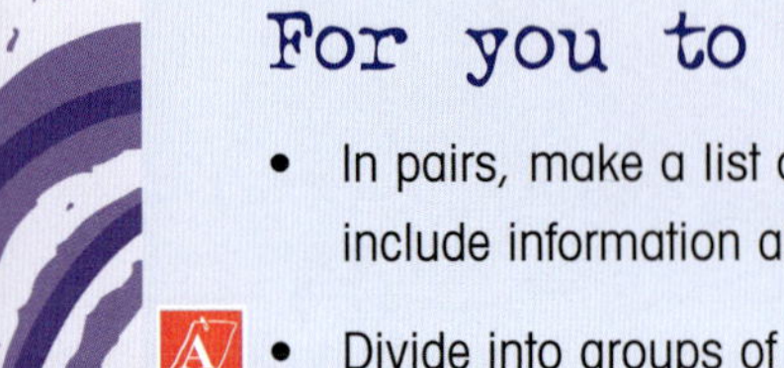

## For you to try

- In pairs, make a list of the things that you should check for when planning and preparing a meal. You should include information about the food and the way that the food will be handled.
- A Divide into groups of four or five students. Each group should plan a simple meal that you can prepare at schoc Each student should bring something that is needed to prepare the meal in the next class. After you have prepared the meal, share it with other groups. Which groups prepared nutritious meals? Explain why the meal was nutritious.

# Personal health and safety ML

Most people do not like to be sick. They do not like the feeling, and they may live a long way from a health centre or hospital so getting treatment may be very difficult. Children who are sick cannot learn properly and adults who are sick cannot work properly. Also, people who are sick need someone to look after them, so the carer or guardian may not be able to do their normal work.

There are many things that we can do in order to take care of our own health. These are *choices* that we make in order to be healthy. Choosing some behaviour and not others is the main way that we can stay healthy. For example, smoking tobacco is a choice that people make. People who smoke have more health problems than people who do not smoke. Choosing not to smoke is one way of trying to stay healthy.

Health workers say that *prevention is better than cure*. This means that it is better to try to prevent sickness than to wait until the person is sick and then try to make them better. For example, it is better to sleep under a mosquito net to prevent mosquitoes biting you at night than to wait until you get malaria and then go and get treatment. However, if you do get sick, it is important to get treatment quickly and not wait until you get worse.

Something that we can all do is to collect true information before we make choices about what we do.

# PROMOTING PERSONAL HEALTH

**My personal health plan – the choices I make**

Bath every day

Brush teeth every day

Comb and wash hair regularly

Keep fingernails short and clean

Keep nose clean (no 'number 11' coming down)

Treat sores and keep them covered

Take regular exercise

Eat a balanced diet and do not eat 'rubbish' foods

Do not chew betel nut with lime

Do not smoke tobacco

Avoid drinking too much alcohol (when I am old enough to drink)

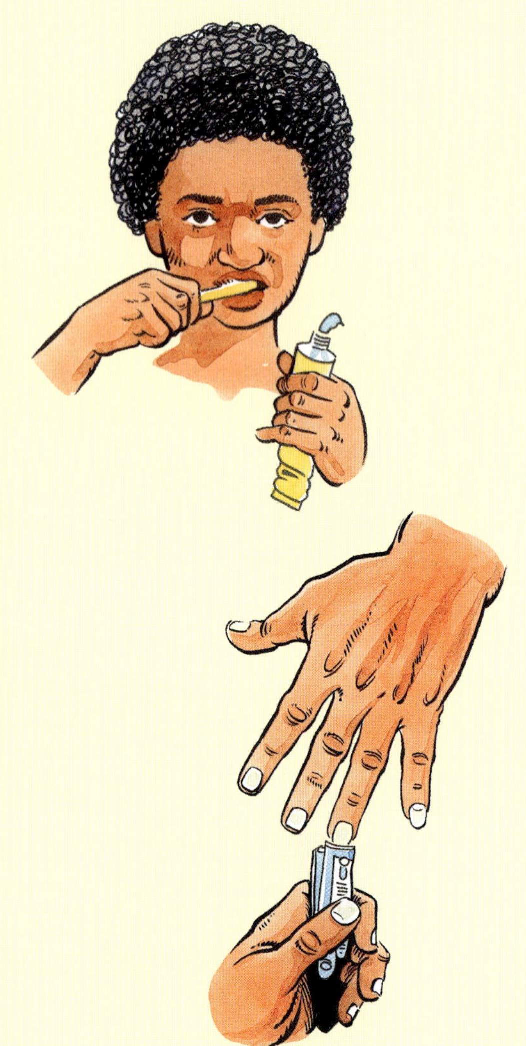

If you want to find out more about taking care of your own health, you can get information from the following places:

- the local community health centre or hospital
- radio, newspapers, books and other media like television
- parents and teachers
- church groups
- women's groups

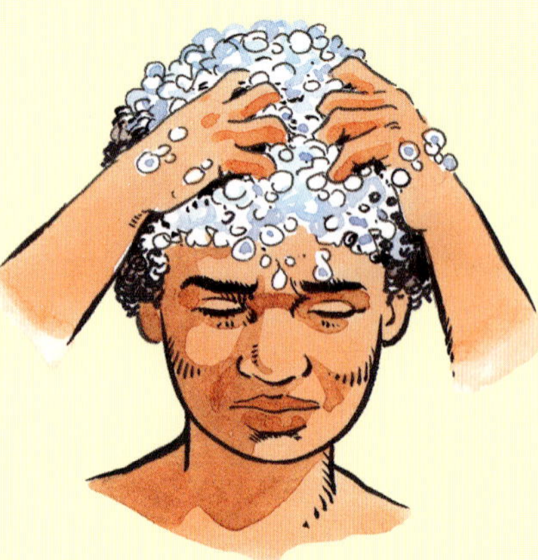

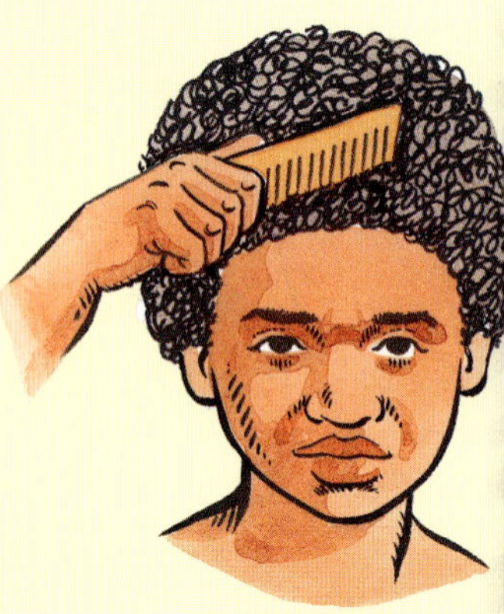

## For you to try

- Write out your own personal health plan like the one above. Add some different points that are not included in the list above.

  Show your plan to one of your classmates.

  Tell them which choices on the plan are hardest to follow.

  Explain why some choices are hard to follow.

# COMMON ILLNESSES AND DISEASES

Even though we try to prevent ourselves from getting sick, there will be times when we do get sick. We need to understand the causes of the sickness and what we can do in order to get better.

Most common illnesses are caused by small living things called **germs** or **microbes** like **bacteria** and **viruses.** Some microbes can make us sick when they get inside our bodies or get on our skin. For example:

- Tinea or ringworm is caused by a fungus that grows on our skin. It can be spread by direct contact and by sharing clothes, towels and bed sheets. Ringworm is also called **grille** or sipoma.
- **Malaria** is caused by germs that are carried by some mosquitoes that usually bite at night.
- Colds and influenza are caused by microbes such as viruses.
- **Gastroenteritis** can be caused by bacteria, viruses or **food poisoning.** People usually have vomiting and diarrhoea. It can be spread by food and drink, cups and plates.
- **Dengue** is caused by viruses that are carried by mosquitoes that bite in the daytime. Dengue is also known as breakbone fever because of the pain that is felt in the joints.

## For you to try

- Write a story about personal health or hygiene with the title 'Prevention is better than cure'.
- If you live in a remote area where it is hard to obtain things like soap, combs and toothbrushes, make a list of any alternatives that you know that are made from local materials. You may need to talk to older people to get this information and show you how to make them. Copy and complete the following table to help you.

| Material | Part of body to clean | How is it used? |
|---|---|---|
| Seaweed | Teeth | Take off hard covering of seaweed by rubbing between palms — rub on teeth |
| | | |

- How can you encourage other people to take care of themselves and make sensible choices based on true information?

- **Tuberculosis** or TB is caused by bacteria and affects the lungs. People with TB lose weight and spit blood. It is spread by coughing.
- **Typhoid** is caused by bacteria and affects the **digestive system**. It is spread by food and drink.
- **Scabies** is caused by a little animal called a *mite* that lives in the skin. It is often found between the fingers and is very itchy. It moves from person to person by direct contact.
- **Sexually transmitted infections** can be caused by bacteria and viruses and are spread by sexual contact. Examples are: syphilis, gonorrhoea, donovanosis and HIV/AIDS.

However, not all microbes are harmful and some are useful. For example, when we make bread, we use a microbe called *yeast*. We cannot make bread without yeast and the yeast does not make us sick. Yeast is also used to make beer and wine.

Microbes are also used in the production of tea, coffee, cocoa, cheese and yoghurt. Another example is the antibiotic medicine **penicillin**, which is made from mould called penicillium.

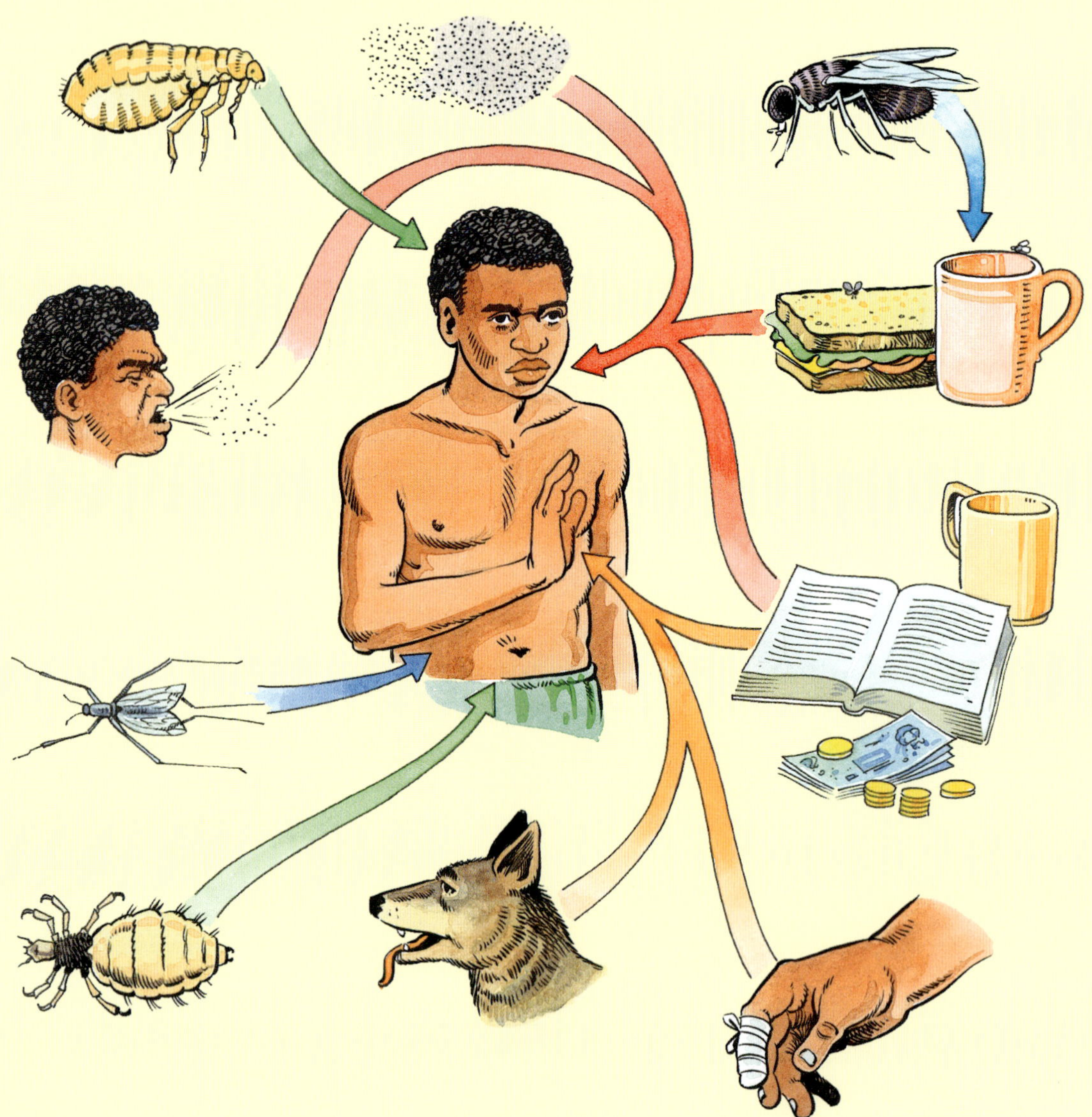

**Ways that microbes enter the body**

We know when we get sick because we can feel or see certain **signs** and **symptoms**. For example, if you have tummy ache or gastroenteritis, you might have diarrhoea and vomiting, you might have a temperature or a fever, and you might not feel like eating. But if you do not drink then you may become dehydrated and may faint.

It is very important to drink plenty of liquids even if you do not feel like eating. Babies and small children can die if they are very dehydrated and so they must be given plenty of liquids. Babies should be given plenty of breast milk, and children can be given sugar water. You can make sugar water by adding one heaped teaspoon of sugar to a big cup of clean water (do not add salt).

**Table 1 Some common illnesses and diseases**

- malaria
- colds and influenza
- gastroenteritis
- dengue
- tuberculosis
- grille
- sexual diseases
- typhoid

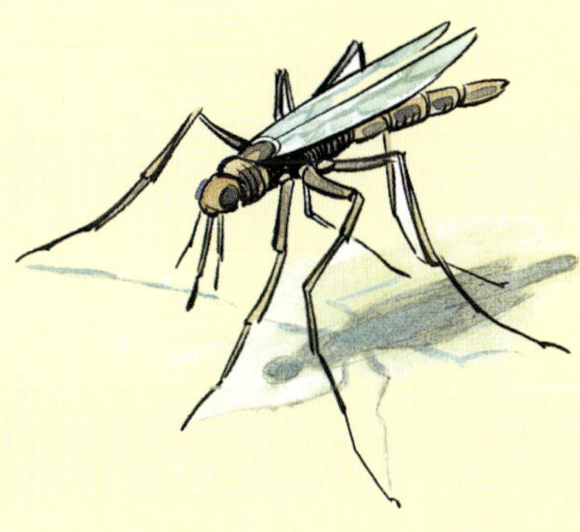

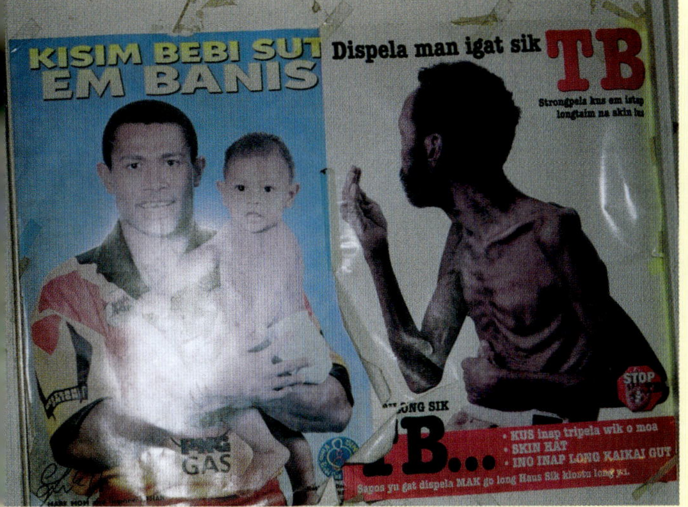


**Table 2 How illnesses are spread**

- germs like bacteria and viruses
- eating contaminated food
- drinking contaminated water
- sharing cups and other utensils
- coughing – can spread germs in the air
- insects like mosquitoes can spread some germs
- unclean home and environment
- sexual contact
- inherited from parents

# PROTECTION FROM ILLNESSES

There are many ways that we are able to protect ourselves from illnesses.

**Ways to protect ourselves from illness**

- Wash and keep hands clean – especially after going to the toilet and before touching food.
- Wash eating and cooking utensils with hot water.
- Keep the home and the surroundings clean.
- Sleep under mosquito nets if there is malaria in the area.
- Cover your mouth when coughing and sneezing.
- Wash clothes, towels and bed sheets regularly and dry in the sun.
- Always follow instructions when taking medicine – especially when taking antibiotics or medicine for malaria.
- Cooked food should be eaten when it is hot. Do not eat cooked food that has been kept warm for many hours. Keep food covered.
- Have only safe sexual contact.

## For you to try

- Copy tables 1 and 2 on page 71. Using the information in the diagram 'Ways that microbes enter the body', draw lines to match the common illness or disease with the way that it is spread.
- Choose two diseases as follows: (1) a disease that is common in your area (2) a disease that spreads rapidly from person to person. For each illness, list the signs and symptoms then describe how the illness can be prevented and how people can protect themselves.
- Find out about an illness that is inherited from our parents.

# ML RISKS AND HAZARDS

A **risk** is a behaviour that can have a bad effect on our health or well-being. For example, if you are riding on the back of a truck, then there is the risk that you will fall off and hurt yourself. If you hold on carefully then you can reduce the risk and the activity becomes much safer. We need to understand the level of risk of a particular activity. Some activities have high risk and some have low risk.

A **hazard** is a danger that we find in our surroundings. For example, a fire is a hazard because we can burn ourselves or burn down a building. A flooded river is a hazard because if we try to cross a flooded river we may get carried away and drown. Roads are also a hazard because there is a danger that we will be hit by a truck or a car.

There are different *levels* of danger with each hazard. Some hazards have a high level of danger and some have a low level of danger. We need to understand the level of danger of each hazard. We need to know how we can reduce the danger because of the way that we behave.

There are many risks and hazards to our health and well-being at school, at home and in the community:

- not enough clean water
- no proper toilets
- no proper rubbish disposal
- overcrowding in buildings
- poor ventilation in buildings
- playing with dangerous animals or plants, for example, sea urchins
- playing in and around water – rivers, lakes and the sea – swimming, fishing, using canoes
- lighting a fire, using fire, moving around a fire
- fighting
- drunkenness
- rape

## For you to try

- Using the list of risks and hazards, separate these into two groups: risks and hazards.
- In your class, brainstorm a list of several hazardous situations. Divide into groups of four or five students. Divide the list of hazardous situations among the groups. Each group describes the level of danger of each hazardous situation. Each group reports back to the whole class.

# Community health

When many people get the same sickness we say that there is a health problem in the community. For example, if people leave rubbish in the wrong place then there may be lots of blue flies and rats. If people do not wash their hands properly and keep food covered then we may see people with *diarrhoea* in the community. If children do not get enough of the right kind of food then there may be **malnutrition** in children in the community. Malnutrition is very common in Papua New Guinea. If people do not wash their bodies, clothes, towels and bed sheets regularly then we may see many people with ringworm.

Health problems in the community have different causes and ways of being carried from person to person.

Some health problems may be caused by *germs* like bacteria and viruses.

Some germs may be *carried by animals* such as insects and rats.

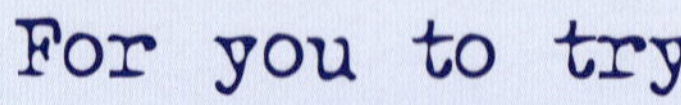


- Choose a high risk situation. Say how you would behave in order to avoid this situation or to lower the risk.
- In groups, choose a hazardous situation in your school, home or community. Plan and carry out an activity to improve understanding and deal with the hazard. Think about using posters, drama and role plays, music.
- A Design a poster or some other awareness campaign to get people to do the right thing – for example, to get people to use toilets properly, or to put rubbish in the right place.

Some health problems may come from the ***surroundings***. For example, drinking dirty water, swimming or playing in dirty water, or breathing dirty air.

Some health problems may come because of the way that people ***behave***. For example, drinking beer, chewing betel nut or because of their sexual behaviour.

| Health problem in the community | Cause of this problem | How to prevent this problem |
|---|---|---|
| Malnutrition – children who are underweight, or children who look fat but have thin muscles in their arms and legs | Not getting enough of the right kind of food | |
| Diarrhoea | Dirty water (pollution) | |
| Breathing problems | Smoke from fires, tobacco smoke, dirty air | |
| Drunkenness | Too much alcohol | |
| HIV and AIDS | Sexual behaviour | |

## WAYS OF CARING FOR THE COMMUNITY TO STAY HEALTHY

There are many ways that we can care for the community so that we can all be healthier.

- Encourage everyone to use the toilet and keep toilets clean.
- Put all rubbish in bins. Keep bins covered with a lid and empty bins regularly.
- In the village, burn and bury rubbish and cover with soil.
- Keep all rubbish out of water supplies like creeks, rivers and wells.
- Keep water tanks covered so that mosquitoes cannot breed.
- Remove the places where mosquitoes breed, like old tins, coconuts and tyres.
- Make a compost heap for dead leaves.

# PEOPLE AND PLACES THAT HELP THE COMMUNITY TO STAY HEALTHY

There are many people and places that help people to stay healthy:

- community health workers
- Maternal and Child Health Clinics (MCH)
- health-promoting schools
- doctors and nurses
- dentists
- church groups

*Recommended immunisation programme in Papua New Guinea*

| Immunisation or vaccination | Age 1st | 2nd | 3rd | Disease prevented |
|---|---|---|---|---|
| BCG | Birth | Age 3 | Age 13 | Tuberculosis |
| Hepatitis B | Birth | 1 month | 3 months | Hepatitis B |
| Triple antigen | 1 month | 2 months | 3 months | Diphtheria, whooping cough, tetanus (lockjaw) |
| Sabin | Birth | 1 month | 2 months | Polio (4th immunisation at 3 months) |
| Pigbel | 1 month | 2 months | 3 months | Pigbel (immunise again at age 7 and 13) |
| Measles | 6 months | 9 months | | Measles |
| Tetanus toxoid | 7 years | 13 years | | Tetanus (lockjaw) |
| Tetanus toxoid (mother) | Each pregnancy | Each pregnancy | Each pregnancy | Tetanus (lockjaw) |

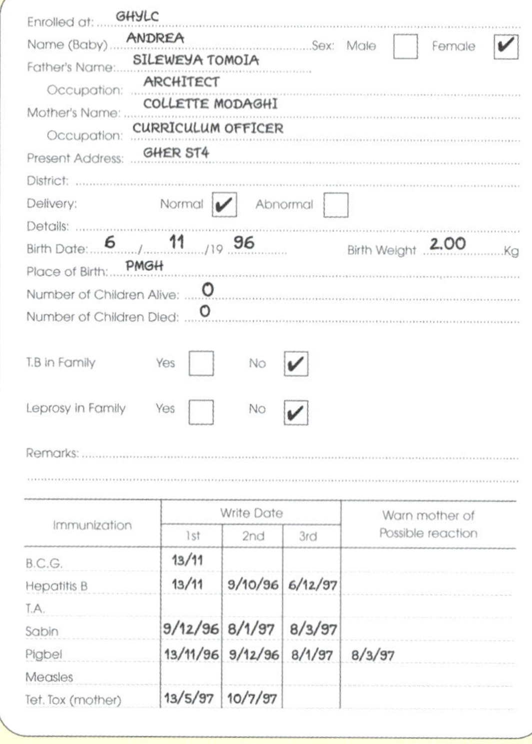

Enrolled at: GHYLC

Name (Baby) ANDREA Sex: Male ☐ Female ☑

Father's Name: SILEWEYA TOMOIA

Occupation: ARCHITECT

Mother's Name: COLLETTE MODAGHI

Occupation: CURRICULUM OFFICER

Present Address: GHER ST4

District:

Delivery: Normal ☑ Abnormal ☐

Details:

Birth Date: 6 / 11 /19 96 Birth Weight 2.00 Kg

Place of Birth: PMGH

Number of Children Alive: 0

Number of Children Died: 0

T.B in Family Yes ☐ No ☑

Leprosy in Family Yes ☐ No ☑

Remarks:

| Immunization | Write Date 1st | 2nd | 3rd | Warn mother of Possible reaction |
|---|---|---|---|---|
| B.C.G. | 13/11 | | | |
| Hepatitis B | 13/11 | 9/10/96 | 6/12/97 | |
| T.A. | | | | |
| Sabin | 9/12/96 | 8/1/97 | 8/3/97 | |
| Pigbel | 13/11/96 | 9/12/96 | 8/1/97 | 8/3/97 |
| Measles | | | | |
| Tet. Tox (mother) | 13/5/97 | 10/7/97 | | |

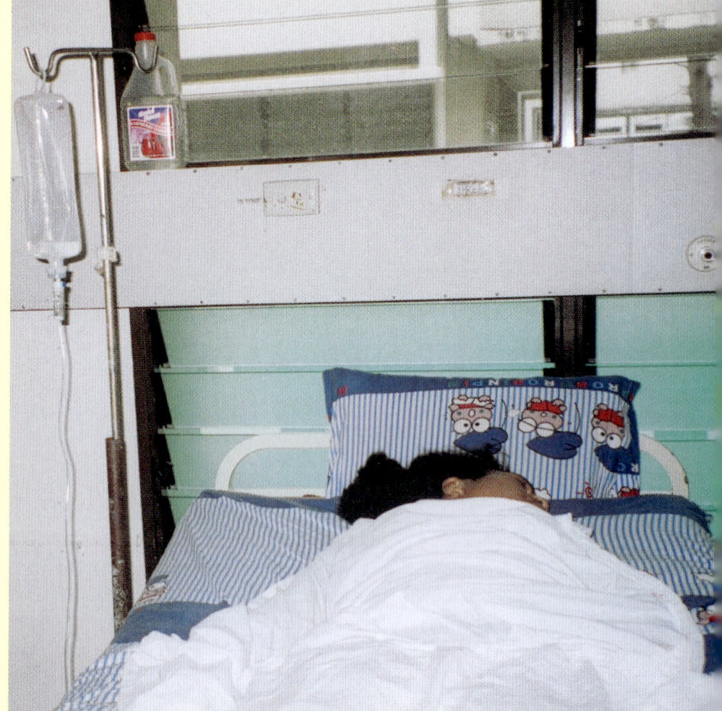

One of the ways that we can help people to be healthy is by **immunisation**. By giving **injections** or **vaccinations** we prevent people from getting sick from some diseases. It is important that children and mothers get their vaccinations at the right time. Children's vaccinations should be written down in their record book so that parents and health workers can check that a child has been immunised.

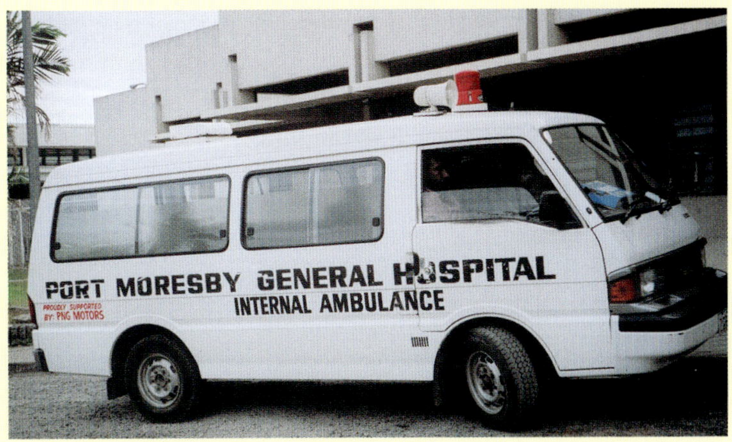


Doctors, nurses and other health workers sometimes count the number of people who are sick to find out more about the problem and then help the community to do something about it. For example, if many people are having the same sickness then there must be a reason. When health workers find this reason then advice or help can be given to the community to help to solve the problem.

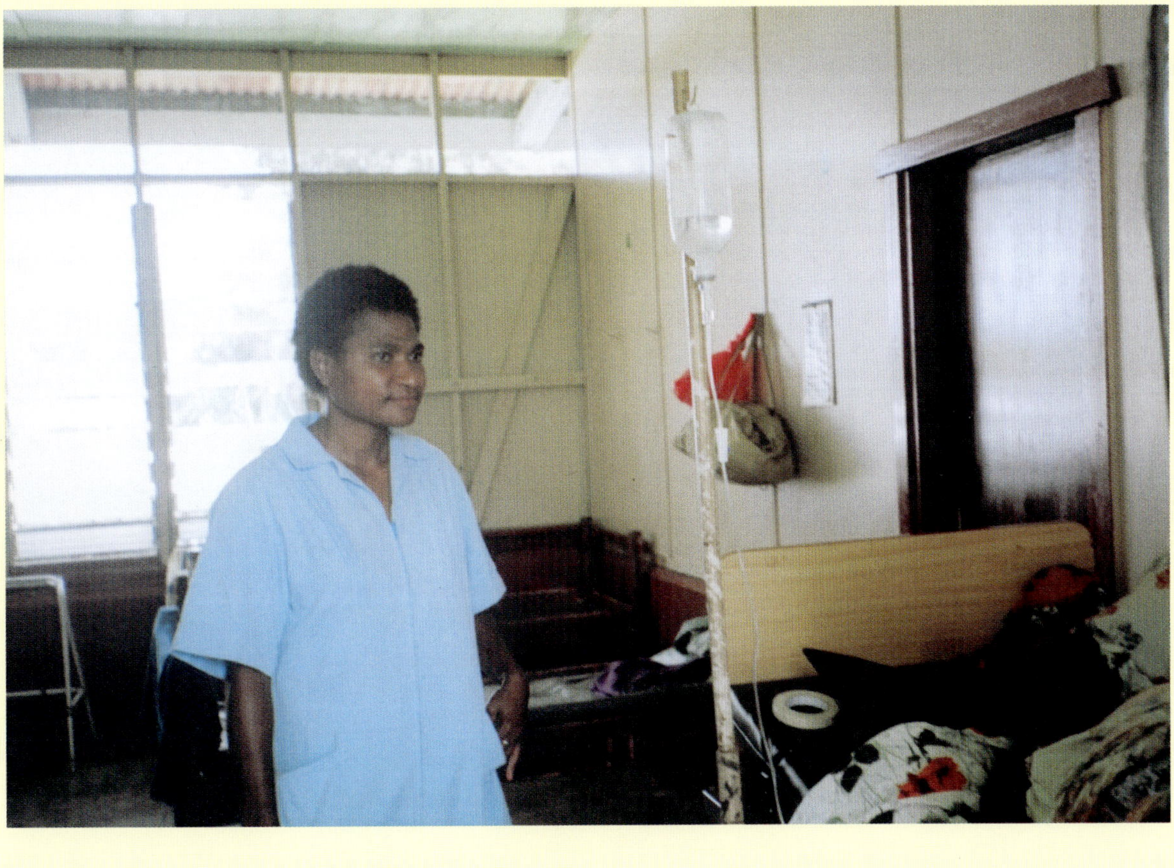

## For you to try

- Copy the table on page 75 and complete the third column to show how health patterns can be prevented.

- Copy and complete the following table. Make a list of health concerns and say where each problem is happening – remember this may be happening in more than one place. Two examples have been done for you.

| Health concerns or problems where I live | School | Home | Community |
|---|---|---|---|
| Blue flies breeding in rubbish | | | X |
| People going to the toilet in the bush | X | | X |
| | | | |
| | | | |

- What can you do to help to reduce the problems that you listed in your table above?
- Find out about the people and places that help you to stay healthy. Where are these places? What do the people do who work there (use the list on page 76)?

- Work in small groups. Make up a story about a community that has a health problem. First talk about the problem and the reasons for it. Then work out what the community can do to change and try to make things better. Act out your story for others to see. What are the main messages of your story? How can you improve your story?
- Look at the picture (right) and explain how the behaviour of the people can affect the health of the whole community.
- Look at the recommended immunisation program in PNG and Andrea's record of immunisation shown on page 76. Comment on whether Andrea has received all her immmunisations at the recommended time. Is she in danger of catching any diseases because she has not been immunised?

# The use of drugs

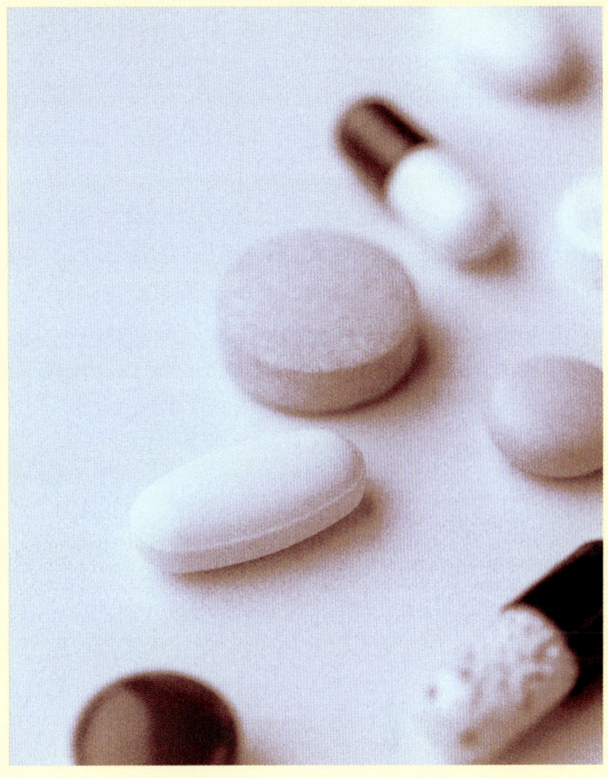

When we get sick we can sometimes take *medicine* to help us get better. For example, if you have a bad headache then you can take *Asprin, Aspro Clear, Panadol or Paracetamol.* These medicines are *pain killers* and will take away the pain. If you have a cough then you may buy cough medicine. Aspirin and cough medicine are both medicines that can be bought in stores.

If you are sick and visit the aid post or hospital, the health worker may give you some medicine to help you get better. For example, if you have malaria, you may be given *chloroquine*, and if you have an infection like a sore on your foot or leg, you may be given an **antibiotic** like *penicillin.* Some of these medicines can be given in the form of an *injection.*

All of these medicines are examples of *drugs.* A drug is any chemical substance that changes the body in some way. Medicines are drugs that change the body by helping the body to get better and to make you feel better. The *type* of drug and the *amount* of the drug that we take are important. Using the wrong drug or using too much can make a person sick.

Some drugs are called *prescription drugs.* This means that we can only use this drug if we have been given a special piece of paper, called a **prescription**, from a doctor. When you take this prescription to a pharmacy, the **pharmacist** or chemist chooses the correct drugs written on the prescription.

Prescription drugs are strong drugs or drugs that can cause a problem if they are not used in the correct way. We should take these drugs only when the doctor tells us to take them. Having a prescription helps to control the use of the drug and so protects people who could be harmed if they do not use the drug properly. For example, some antibiotics like penicillin and some pain killers are prescription drugs. When you take antibiotic tablets you have to take them for many days, and it is important to remember to do this.

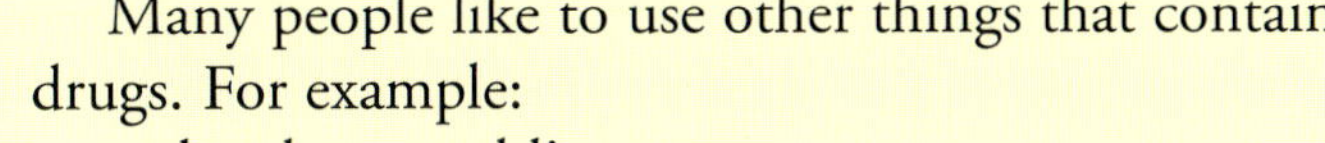

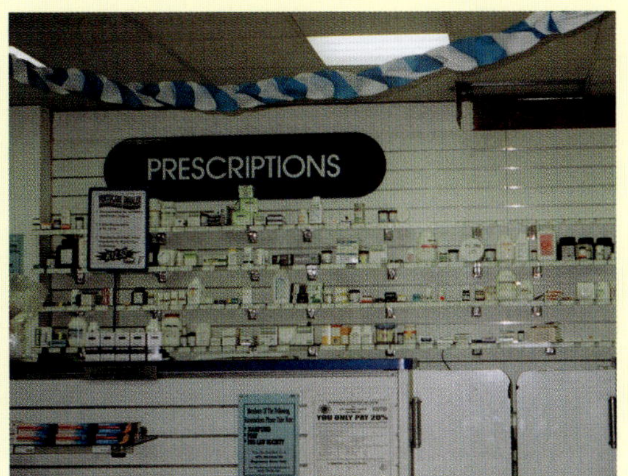


Many people like to use other things that contain drugs. For example:

- betel nut and lime
- tobacco – including 'brus' and cigarettes
- alcohol – beer, wine and spirits
- tea – which contains a drug called caffeine
- coffee – which contains a drug called caffeine
- 'cola' drinks – which contain a drug called caffeine

All of these are *legal* drugs. People like to drink tea and coffee and the drug they contain (caffeine) does not usually harm them, so people do not need stop using it. 'Cola' drinks are not harmful if we do not drink too much, although they do contain a lot of sugar, which can make people overweight.

Although they are legal, you cannot use some drugs until you are an adult. For example, you cannot buy or drink alcohol until you are eighteen years old. In many countries children and young people under the age of eighteen are not allowed to buy cigarettes. This is because smoking tobacco and drinking alcohol can both be *harmful* to our health. Chewing betel nut and lime can also be harmful to our health.

Some drugs are *illegal* drugs. It is against the law to have illegal drugs, and when the police catch people with illegal drugs they can be taken to court and punished. All illegal drugs can be *harmful* to our health. Examples of illegal drugs are:

- cannabis and marijuana
- amphetamines
- heroin
- cocaine

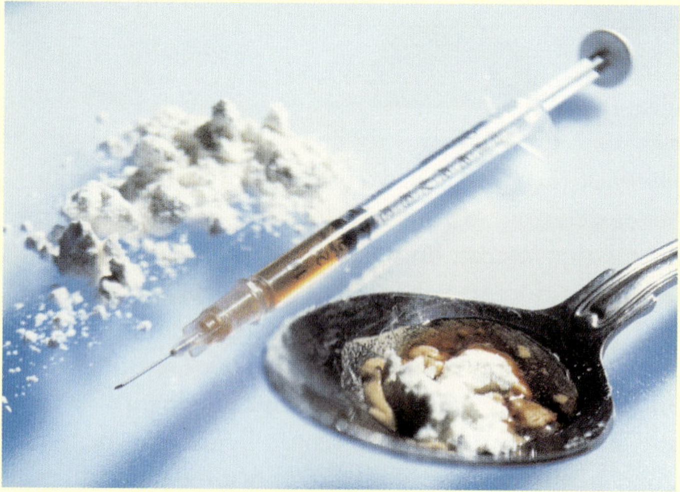

**Heroin is very harmful to your health.**

**Cannabis or marijuana is illegal.**

# EFFECTS OF HARMFUL DRUGS

Chewing betel nut and mustard is important in many parts of Papua New Guinea and is part of the culture of many places. However, chewing betel nut with lime for many years can cause bad sores called *cancer.* This cancer can develop in the mouth and cause the cheeks to be eaten away, leaving a big hole that does not heal. It is very painful and in serious cases the person may die.

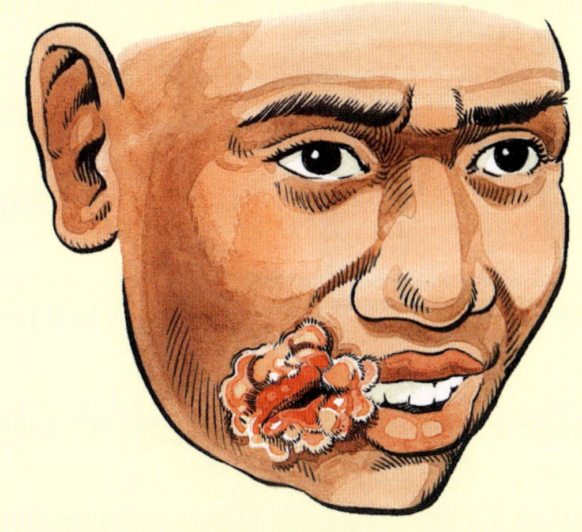

**Cancer caused by chewing betel nut with lime.**

Smoking tobacco is also common in Papua New Guinea and some people are able to grow their own tobacco. Unfortunately, when people smoke tobacco they can get a number of diseases, including lung diseases like lung cancer. Smoking is the cause of more sickness in the world than any other reason, so if people stop smoking a lot of sickness will be prevented.

Tobacco contains a drug called *nicotine* which is *addictive*. This means that once people start to smoke they find it very hard to stop, even though they may know that smoking can make them sick. For this reason it is best to never start smoking. In many countries in the world, cigarettes have a warning on the packet telling people that smoking can damage their health. In many countries, including Papua New Guinea, smoking is also not allowed in public buildings and on aeroplanes.

Marijuana is a plant that grows in Papua New Guinea and is sometimes called cannabis. It is a drug that is smoked and can cause the same health problems as smoking tobacco.

Amphetamines, cocaine and heroin are drugs that are used in some countries but are not commonly found in Papua New Guinea.

## For you to try

- Find out about the law in Papua New Guinea in relation to cigarettes and smoking.

  Do packets of cigarettes have a health warning?
  Can children buy cigarettes in Papua New Guinea?
  Are there places where smoking is not allowed?

- Gather information about different kinds of drugs and complete the following table.

| Drug | Source—where does it come from? | How it affects the body |
|---|---|---|
| | | |
| | | |

## OTHER HARMFUL EFFECTS OF DRUGS

People who use drugs regularly may find that some, or all, of the following things happen:

- They spend a lot of money on drugs so there is not enough money in the family for important things like food, clothes and school fees.
- They find it hard to work or to do their job properly.
- They sometimes have mental problems.
- They feel that they have lost control of part of their life so they lose self-respect, and other people may also lose respect for them.
- They have family breakdown.
- They do not always eat properly and so they lose weight and become very skinny.

## REASONS FOR TAKING DRUGS

People take drugs for many different reasons. Some of these are health reasons and others are not health reasons. For example:

- to prevent illnesses
- to cure a disease
- to feel good
- for celebrations and relaxation
- to feel better
- to feel part of the group
- to avoid feeling sad or depressed
- to relax and forget social and family problems
- to know what it feels like
- because they feel shy or embarrassed
- because they think that it is a 'grown-up' thing to do
- because parents or other family members influence them

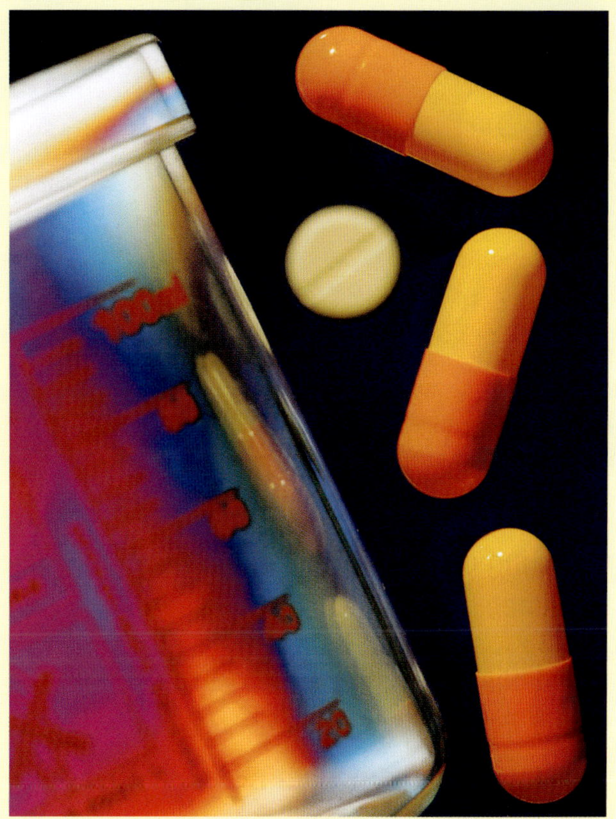

### For you to try

- Write two or three paragraphs saying why you think people start to take drugs.
- What are your views on taking drugs?
- Role models are people who are well known and who are admired and respected because of their achievements and the way they behave. Can you identify someone who is well known in your community or in the country who is a role model and can influence young people not to take harmful drugs?

# Living and Working Together

## Chapter Summary

*In this chapter you will have an opportunity to:*

- ✔ Find out what it means to be a positive member of a group
- ✔ Find out about the way that we make decisions
- ✔ Find out about what makes a good leader
- ✔ Describe the rules and laws that we follow at school, in the family and in the community
- ✔ Identify and describe standards of behaviour in different groups and places

## Syllabus references

**Strand:** Living and working together
**Sub-strands:** Making choices, good and fair leaders, rule of law, respecting rights and freedoms

**Outcomes:**

6.5.1 Outline what it means to be a positive member of a family, clan or community

6.5.2 Describe the process of making decisions

6.5.3 Describe the qualities of a good and fair leader

6.5.4 Describe familiar rules and laws of the community, families and schools

6.5.5 Describe community standards of behaviour that support rights and freedoms

## Key facts

- People have different qualities. These qualities can help them to be a good and useful member of a group.
- We can make good decisions by following certain steps.
- There are different influences on the way that we make decisions.
- To be a good and fair leader the person must have certain qualities.
- Rules and laws guide our behaviour.
- Rules and laws help to protect us and keep us safe.
- People have rights and freedoms and we must also respect the rights and freedoms of other people.

# Making choices

## QUALITIES OF A GOOD MEMBER OF A GROUP ML

All people are different and behave in different ways. We say that people have different *qualities*. For example, some people are very *reliable*. When they say that they are going to do something we know that they will do it. Some people are *unreliable*. When they say that they are going to do something we are not sure if they will do it or not. Some people are *caring* and try to think about other people before they do or say something. Some people are *selfish* and think mainly about themselves and do not care what happens to other people.

What do you think are the qualities that help you to be a positive member of a group?

- reliable
- honest
- trustworthy
- caring
- kind
- hard-working
- helpful
- loyal or faithful
- fair

What other qualities can you add to this list?

**Nora Vagi Brash – a notable female writer**

### For you to try

- Choose five qualities from the list above, or others that you can think of. For each quality give some examples of the kind of behaviour that you would like to see in a member of your family or community.

## VALUES

The qualities that we expect people to have also tell us about our **values**. Our values are the things that we say or think are important.

People show their values by the way that they behave, not just by what they say. For example, when we value *honesty* we do not steal from other people, cheat or tell lies. At the same time we do not want other people to steal from us, cheat or tell lies to us. If we *say* that we value honesty but we do not *behave* in ways that show we are honest, then people will not believe what we say and will not respect us.

Values come from the things that people believe are good and right and true. We all begin to learn values when we are children and we continue throughout our lives. Parents and teachers help children to develop the values that are accepted in the community. We also learn values from being a member of a church or a religion and from other groups in the community. We show our values by the way that we behave, not just by what we say. The values that we use to make decisions are shown below:

### Respect

Respect for myself and others
Respect for laws and for authority
Respect for private and public property—the things that belong to other people and the community

### Honesty

Being fair and trustworthy
Being reliable and dependable
Knowing and admitting when other people are dishonest

### Obligations—things that you must do

Obligations to your family and community
Being open-minded, ready to listen, not too quick to judge other people
Being interested in the community and prepared to ask questions

### Concern

Being kind and considerate and understanding the feelings of other people
Being cooperative and accepting that people are different and that there can be more than one way of doing things
Sharing in decision-making

### Dedication

Knowing and understanding what is happening in the community
Taking part in community activities
Helping the community before helping yourself—being civic-minded

## Justice

Being fair and treating people equally
Respecting the rights of other people
Letting the law do the job that it has to do

As we grow up, we learn how to become a member of different groups who share the same values. We learn to cooperate with other people and other people then accept us.

### For you to try

- What are the five most important values? Give reasons for your choice.
- Show your list of values to other students in your class and ask them what they think. Look for similarities and differences in your lists. Your teacher may want to collect ideas from each group and put them on the blackboard.
- What happens to people who do not learn to be part of a group or community?
-  Describe some practical activities that you can do to show the values in your behaviour.

## MAKING DECISIONS

When we are babies we have no decisions to make. The adults who take care of us make all the decisions for us. As we grow up we learn to make decisions every day of our lives.

Some of these decisions are easy to make. For example, today you may have decided what clothes to wear, what food to eat and how much time to spend with your friends. These are usually easy decisions to make, and the result of the decision may not be very important. For example, if you did not spend much time with your friends today then you may be able to spend time with them tomorrow.

Other decisions can be much harder to make and the result can be much more important. For example, if you decide to do something dangerous then you may hurt yourself and other people. If you decide to do something illegal then you may get into trouble with the police.

As we become adults, we learn to make important decisions in our lives.

## INFLUENCES ON DECISION-MAKING

Many things may affect or influence the important decisions that we make. These are some of the questions that we can ask so that we can understand the things that may influence our decision-making. Remember, influences can be positive or negative.

- Do I have enough knowledge or information to make this decision?
- What do *I* think and feel about this decision?
- What do *others* think and feel?
- What about my values and the values of my family and community? How do they affect my decision?
- Are my friends or peers putting pressure on me?
- Are my parents putting pressure on me?

- Will my decision have an effect on other members of the community?
- Is there a conflict between modern and traditional values?

## For you to try

**Mrs Pilou**

Mrs Pilou graduated from the University of Papua New Guinea with a diploma in Basic Accounting and Business Studies. The following year she was employed by the Steamships Joint Venture in Vanimo as an Assistant Accountant. She showed great interest in her job and worked very closely with the other staff and workers. She had a very pleasant attitude and her dedication towards her work was very much appreciated by the General Manager of the company. During working days Mrs Pilou made sure that all her documents and records were in good order. Mrs Pilou worked there for a year and then she was sponsored by the company for further studies at the Business College in Port Moresby.

**Mr Sese**

Mr Sese was the newly elected chairman of Bronto Community School. At first he carried out his work well and the parents and citizens were pleased and encouraged him to continue. They thought that he was the right person to take up the position. Later that year he changed completely. He stopped calling meetings and when the headteacher called meetings at the school he always gave excuses. The real reason was that Mr Sese was deeply involved in gambling. The parents and citizens found out that Mr Sese had used up a K500 cheque from the school subsidy fund, so they removed him and decided to elect a new chairman. Everyone in the community heard about this and was telling stories about him.

- Compare the two case studies. What are the different decisions that were made by Mrs Pilou and Mr Sese? How did their decisions affect the end result? What do you think will happen to Mrs Pilou and Mr Sese in the future?
- Think about an important decision that you have made in your life. Choose one influence that affected the way that you made your decision. Was the influence positive or negative? If it was negative, how could it be changed?

## STEPS IN DECISION-MAKING

Making decisions about important things that happen in your life can be quite difficult. This is one way to help you make decisions. You need to carry out each step before moving on to the next one. It can be very helpful to write down the answers to these questions because it makes you think more carefully, and then you can compare the possible results from different choices.

1 What is the *issue* or the *problem*?
2 What are the *options* or *choices* that I can make?
3 What are the *good things* and the *bad things* that can happen as a result of *each* option?
4 Make your decision after thinking about the *possibilities*.
5 How do I *feel* about the choices that I have made?

After you have made your decision and you have seen the result, the last step is to think about the decision and decide if it was a good one. If your decision was a good one then you will probably feel more confident about making decisions in the future. If your decision was a bad one then you need to try to find out why it was not a good decision so that you do not make the same mistake again.

# Good and fair leaders

Sometimes adults tell young people that they are 'the leaders of tomorrow'. This may be true. However, we cannot all be leaders. For this reason, when we choose our leaders it is the job of the leader to represent us and speak for all of us.

The people who choose the leader are not just the 'followers' but expect the leader to behave in certain ways. For example, when we elect people to be members of a committee or to be politicians, we expect them to represent and serve the people who elected them. Leaders should not just put their own point of view or help themselves and their own family or clan.

Being a good and fair leader is not easy and not everyone can do it. We should respect leaders, but leaders also need to behave in ways that earn the respect of the people.

## For you to try

- List some of the important matters in your life that you may have to make decisions about in the future.
-  Think about a situation in which you have to make a decision. Using the decision-making steps, write a description of how you will make your decision.
- Discuss with a partner how you used the steps for decision-making.

## QUALITIES OF A GOOD AND FAIR LEADER

- Good role model for others to follow
- Interested in helping other people
- Honest, loyal and humble
- Patient
- Tolerant of other people
- Can solve problems peacefully
- Knows and understands people in the community
- Listens to other people
- Respected by people in the community

**Dr Rose Kekedo – the first Papua New Guinean woman to head a government department**

## For you to try

- Think of some more qualities of a good leader that you can add to the list above.
- How do students become leaders in your school? Describe the steps in the process.
- When leaders are chosen or elected, what happens when they do not do their job properly? How can we help leaders to do their job? How can leaders be changed?
- A Think of a leader that you know at your school or in your community. Describe the qualities that make that person a good leader. Explain why you think these are positive qualities.

### Jailing of magistrate regrettable: Numapo

By Moresi Ruahma a

Chief Magistrate John Numapo yesterday described the jailing of senior magistrate Rakatani Mataio by the National Court as an 'unfortunate' thing.

'He (Mataio) was one of the good magistrates who made his way up as a local level magistrate and being in the magisterial services for 27 years,' Mr Numapo said.

Over the years, Mr Mataio travelled long distance from his village to Port Moresby to work because he faced housing problems.

Mr Numapo said no one was above the law and he (Mataio) has been found guilty and convicted by a court of law and must serve his penalty.

'I will be recommending to the Judicial and Legal Services for his dismissal,' he said.

Mr Numapo was commenting on a report in *The National* that said Mr Mataio was sentenced on Friday to prison for six years after being convicted of receiving bribes from a complainant.

- Leaders in PNG do not always show the qualities that are expected. Make up your own list of qualities that you think magistrates should have.

# Rules and laws ML

All communities have *rules* and *laws* that show people the way that they should behave and make it easier for people to live together in the community. Rules and laws may be different in different places. For example, if you have friends in other schools, you may find that some of their school rules are different to yours. Families sometimes have different rules about what children can do.

When people follow the rules or laws then there may be *rewards* to encourage people to continue to follow them. When people are caught breaking a rule or a law then there is usually some sort of *punishment* that is intended to stop the person from breaking the rule or the law in the future.

The laws are made by the government and are the same for everybody in the country. If the police catch people who are breaking the law they can take them to court, and the people can be punished.

## ML THE PURPOSE OF RULES AND LAWS

There should always be a reason for having a rule or law and the reason should be clear to all people. When people understand the reason for the rule or the law they are more likely to follow it. Rules and laws should be based on common sense – the things that most people believe to be right or correct.

## ML WHO MAKES RULES AND LAWS?

- Parents, teachers and village elders
- Community level councillors
- Members of the provincial government
- Members of the national government

People who are experienced in making rules understand that it is better to keep them short and simple rather than to have long lists of rules for people to follow. The people who make rules should look at them regularly to make sure that all the rules are still needed. If a rule is not needed then we should get rid of that rule.

| Rule or law | Why do we have this rule or law? |
|---|---|
| Cross the road only where and when it is safe to do so | To prevent people from being injured or killed |
| Everyone in the family should help to do the work that needs to be done – like cooking, cleaning, doing laundry, gardening | |
| Ask permission from other people before you use things belonging to them | |
| Use resources like firewood and paper carefully so that they are not wasted | |
| Take care of things that belong to you and the things that belong to other people | |
| Houses and schools, villages and towns should be kept clean and tidy | |
| Rubbish should be collected and thrown away in the proper place | |
| When people have disagreements these should be solved in ways that are peaceful and fair | |

## For you to try

- Copy and complete the table above. In the second column, include some of the values that show the reason for having the law.
- Make a table with two columns, one for 'Rules' and one for 'Laws'. Under each heading write down some of the rules and laws that you have seen being followed or broken this week.
- Choose one rule or law that you know well. What would happen if we got rid of this rule or law?
- Think of a situation where a new rule or law is needed. Briefly describe the situation and the rule or law that you would introduce.
- Choose one of the following: your family, school, village or community. Make a set of rules for this group. If there is already a set of rules, say how you would improve the rules. Can any of the rules be removed from the list?

# Respecting rights and freedoms

## COMMON STANDARDS OF BEHAVIOUR

When we are babies we can think only about our own needs. We cry when we are hungry or thirsty or if there is something that we want. As we grow up we learn that we cannot always have the things that we want or that we may have to wait before we get the things that we want. We learn to be less selfish and to think more about other people.

### For you to try

- Add some of your own common standards of behaviour to the list on page 93.
- Choose one of the following: your family, school, clan or tribal group. Talk to other members of the group to identify the common standards of behaviour of the group.
- Using the common standards of behaviour that you found in the previous activity, make a list which puts them in order from the ones that people follow most to the ones that people follow least of all.
- A What can we do when people do not follow the behaviour that is expected in the community? Write down some ways that we can improve standards of behaviour in the community.

We learn that the way we behave affects other people. If each person does exactly as they please without thinking about others, this can cause a lot of trouble in the family or in the community. Selfish behaviour can stop other people doing what they want to do.

This means that there has to be a balance between thinking about yourself and thinking about other people. A person has the freedom to do what they want – so long as this does not take away the freedom of other people to do what they want. Over time, many communities have developed common standards of behaviour that help people to live happily together. For example:

- being fair to other people
- being honest and trustworthy
- being peaceful
- respecting each other
- taking part in community activities
- loving and caring for individuals, groups and the community

## For you to try

- Copy and complete the following table of rights, freedoms and responsibilities. Some examples have been done to help you.

| My rights and freedoms | My responsibilities |
|---|---|
| To feel safe everywhere | To help my parents, brothers and sisters |
| To be able to go school | To be on time and follow school rules |
| | |
| | |
| | |
| | |

# Additional Projects and Investigations

## Chapter 1: Relationships

1 Find out more about village constables, luluais and tultuls. When did Papua New Guinea have these? What did they do? Why do we not have them today? Make a poster about luluais and tultuls, with pictures, and display it in your classroom.

2 Ask old people in your community about the times of the village constables, luluais and tultuls.

3 Invite an older person to come to the school to talk to the students about what life was like in previous times. What did people do? How did people live? How were things different then?

If possible, ask them to show you some of things that people used years ago in their homes or in their work, or to show you some old pictures or old papers. Remember that we need to be careful with old things because they can sometimes be easily broken.

4 Find out about Cooperative Societies in your area. If there are any old people who have been members of Cooperative Societies invite them to come and talk to your class.

How did members of the Cooperative Society help each other? What do you think happened to Cooperative Societies? Why do we not see Cooperative Societies in Papua New Guinea today?

5 Put the following in increasing size, from the group with the smallest number of members to the group with the largest number.

clan village nation province family tribe

6 Do you agree or disagree with the following statements? Give reasons for your answer.

- a All people can be placed into groups
- b We use similarities and differences to put people into groups
- c People can belong to more than one group
- d We can always choose which groups we belong to
- e Achievements are not important.

7 **a** Classify the words below into those groups of which we have a choice to be a member, and those groups of which we do not have a choice to be a member.

| | | | | |
|---|---|---|---|---|
| small | clown | son | granddaughter | groups |
| achievements | cousins | daughter | classmates | best friend |

**b** From the same list find the words that are missing from the passage below:

Everybody belongs to different ____________________. For example, if you are a boy then you must also be a ____________________ to your parents, or if you are a girl you must also be a ____________________. As your grandparents get old they may start to forget some things, but they will never forget that you are their grandson or __________________. If you live near your uncles and aunts then you will probably enjoy playing with your ____________________. When you go to school all the other children in your class will be your ____________________. Some of these may be taller than you and others may be ____________________. In many classes there is a boy or girl who makes the other students laugh a lot and he or she is often known as a ________________. Many boys and girls have a ____________________ at school – someone that they really like and play with a lot. Students who get good marks at school and are good at sport are often recognised for their ____________________.

8 Make a table like the one below and list the roles and responsibilities of the people in your school. You can include the teachers and anyone else who comes into the school to help, like parents.

| Person | Roles and responsibilities |
|---|---|
| Head teacher | |
| Deputy | |
| Class teacher | |
| Class captain | |
| Sports captain | |
| Student | |
| | |

9 Classify the following behaviours into those that help to solve problems and that do not help to solve problems.

- Fighting
- Running away
- Admitting that you were wrong
- Telling lies
- Saying that you are sorry
- Trying to discuss sensibly
- Giving in easily
- Blaming somebody else
- Inviting someone to take part in something you know they will like
- Keeping quiet and refusing to talk
- Asking someone who is not involved to help sort out the problem
- Sulking
- Sharing food or a drink with the other person
- Pretending to be really angry when you are not
- Breaking things
- Keeping calm and trying to think carefully
- Ignoring the problem or pretending that nothing is happening
- Telling stories behind the back of the other person

# Chapter 2: Movement and physical activity

1 If you do not have a first aid kit at your school or at home, then collect the things that are needed and make a kit. For example:

- aspirin
- sticking plaster
- dressing strips
- bandages
- disinfectant
- antibiotic powder

If you are able to buy from a wholesaler then you could buy more cheaply. You could buy enough to make up a number of kits and sell these as a fund-raising activity.

2 If you do not know how to give first aid, invite someone to come to the school to teach first aid.

3 Carry out a survey to find out about sports injuries in your school or community. Use a record sheet like the one below.

| Sport | What happened? (Who? Where? When?) | What care can be taken in future? How can this be prevented? |
|---|---|---|
| | | |
| | | |
| | | |
| | | |
| | | |

Make a summary of your findings and tell the rest of the class.

4 If your school does not have a long jump pit, you might like to make one as a project with your teacher. Any school that can get sand from a beach or a river can easily make a sand pit that can be used for the long jump, triple jump and high jump. Parents and citizens could also help with this project.

5 Help to organise some 'keeping fit' activities for particular groups in the community.

6 Plan and carry out a mini-sports competition for children in your community. Do this to help celebrate an important day like Independence Anniversary, your provincial day or Christmas Day.

7 Learn and perform some traditional dancing to celebrate an important day like Independence Anniversary, your provincial day or the end of the school year. You will need to plan and practice for some weeks before the event. People from the local community could be invited to teach the dances and to take part in the celebration.

8 Using the words in the list, find the words that are missing from the passage below. You can use each word only once.

| | | | | |
|---|---|---|---|---|
| exercise | injured | fit | fair | fun |
| fitness | movement | recreation | roles | abilities |

When we take part in games, sports and dance we need to learn a range of ________________ skills. When we learn sequences of movements we need to think about the different ____________________ that people have. Being ____________________ means being able to take part in everyday activities without getting tired. ____________________ and eating the right kind of food help people to be fit. Rules and safety procedures in games and sport help to prevent people being ____________________ and make the game ____________________. Leisure and ____________________ are activities that people do on their own or in groups to have ____________________ and relax, to make new friends, or to develop ______________. In some games and in organised sport, people have different ____________________ and responsibilities.

9 Which of the following skills are important in netball and basketball?
A. Throwing the ball
B. Catching the ball
C. Throwing and catching
D. Dribbling and fielding

10 Floating and sculling in water are important because
A. They help to win swimming races
B. They help to prevent drowning
C. They help people to get good exercise
D. They give good rhythm and coordination

11 In which of the following sports is dribbling an important skill?

A. Netball and softball
B. Cricket and volleyball
C. Rugby and swimming
D. Soccer and basketball

12 Which of the following are skills that are common to both dancing and sport?

A. Rhythm and timing
B. Dribbling and passing
C. Combining movements in a sequence
D. Making decisions quickly

(a) A only
(b) D only
(c) A and B
(d) A and C

13 Which of the following best describes the sequence of skills that you would use in doing the long jump?

A. Do not put your foot over the line
B. Land on your feet and do not touch the sand with any part of your body
C. Run fast toward the take-off point
D. Keep moving forward away from the pit

(a) A, B, C, D
(b) B, A, C, D
(c) C, A, B, D
(d) C, B, A, D

14 What does it mean to be fit?

A. Taking part in activities without feeling tired
B. Getting your breath back quickly after exercise
C. Relaxing your mind and muscles
D. Feeling happy and energetic
E. Getting along well with others

(a) A and B only
(b) A, B, C and D only
(c) B, C, D and E only
(d) A, B, C, D and E

15 Which of the following activities help to promote fitness?

A. Working in the garden and walking
B. Eating the right kind of food and having a good diet
C. Chewing betel nut and smoking tobacco
D. Getting enough sleep and rest

(a) A, B and C only
(b) A, B and D only
(c) A, C and D only
(d) A, B, C and D

16 What is the purpose of rules and safety procedures in sport?

A. To make the game fair for the players
B. To make the game safe for the players
C. To make the game safe for the spectators
D. To make sure that there is a clear winner

(a) A and B only
(b) C and D only
(c) A, B and C only
(d) A, B, C and D

17 Copy and complete the following table. Which of the following are the responsibilities of team members and which are the responsibility of the coach? If something is the responsibility of both player and coach then you can tick both.

| Responsibility | Player | Coach |
| --- | --- | --- |
| Attend training | | |
| Perform to the best of their ability | | |
| Help players to develop their skills and fitness | | |
| Follow instructions | | |
| Turn up for practices and games on time | | |
| Discipline players – tell them when they are doing right or wrong | | |
| Support other players or performers | | |
| Ensure a safe environment to prevent injury | | |
| Report things that may cause danger, accidents or other problems | | |
| Encourage fair play | | |

# Chapter 3: Our culture, lifestyle and values

1 Find out more about the Hiri or the Kula Ring. Which groups of people were involved? What was exchanged? Why were these trading voyages important to the people who took part in them? Do they still take place today?

- Invite someone from Central Province or Milne Bay to come and talk about traditional trade.
- Find out about the Hiri Moale festival in Port Moresby.

2 Find out about the Moka pig-killing ceremony in the Southern Highlands. Write a short story to answer the following: What happens? Who is involved? Why is it important?

3 Invite elders from the community to come and talk about the changes that they have noticed. Which changes do they feel happy about and which changes do they feel unhappy about? What can people do about the changes that are not good changes?

4 Using the words in the list, find the words that are missing from the passage below. You can use each word only once.

| | | | | |
|---|---|---|---|---|
| subsistence | gardens | exchanging | country | barter |
| culture | changes | languages | traditional | trading |

In Papua New Guinea, the ____________________ of the people is still strong and there are many differences in the culture of people from different parts of the ____________________. There are many different kinds of people with different ____________________, cultures and traditions. In many places, people are still living a ____________________ way of life, but there are also many ____________________ taking place. For example, people who grow food in their ____________________, go fishing and hunting, make their own clothing and build houses from bush materials are sometimes called ____________________. When people from different places first moved about, one of the ways that they came to know each other was through ____________________. Trading means ____________________ something you have for something that someone else has, and which you want. When people trade or swap one type of goods for another type of goods, the exchange is sometimes called ____________________.

5 Answer true or false to the following statements.
   a Bride price is an example of a custom that is still important in some parts of PNG.
   b PNG has developed so much that sorcery and magic are no longer important in any community.
   c Making pottery, weaving mats, carving, and making bilums are examples of traditional skills in PNG.
   d It is difficult to tell which province a person is from by looking at their traditional dancing.
   e People in PNG now mostly grow and eat the same kind of food all over the country.
   f All young people in PNG have to go through initiation ceremonies as they grow older.
   g People from different provinces still have different marriage ceremonies.

6 Classify the following cultural symbols according to whether they are made from plants or animals or they are something that we do (some may belong to more than one group).

| Cultural symbol | Plant | Animal | Other (e.g., something that we do) |
|---|---|---|---|
| Necklace – dog's teeth | | | |
| Necklace – Job's tears | | | |
| Necklace – strips of bamboo | | | |
| Shells like kina and toea, bagi and tabu (shell money) | | | |
| Feathers such as Bird of Paradise plumes | | | |
| Bilums – especially the size, shape and colours used | | | |
| Tattoos on the face and other parts of the body | | | |
| Style of dressing | | | |
| Food | | | |
| Language | | | |

7 Do you agree or disagree with the following statements? Give reasons for you answers.
   a New food crops like English cabbage are better than old crops like aibika.
   b Chemical fertilisers and chemicals that kill pests do not cause any problems.
   c Traditional music should be completely replaced by popular music.
   d White rice and white bread are better than brown rice and brown bread.
   e People should not eat 'fast food' like fried chicken and chips regularly because it contains a lot of fat and added salt, which are not good for health.
   f People should be discouraged from wearing traditional dress.

# Chapter 4: Health of Individuals and Population

1 If your school has a tuck shop or canteen, carry out a survey to find out whether it sells good snack foods or 'rubbish' foods. If it sells 'rubbish' foods make some suggestions about other, more healthy foods that could be sold.

If there is no tuck shop or canteen in your school, carry out a survey to find out if there is a need for one.

2 In your class or your school, plan and carry out a long-term project to improve the health of the school or community. For example:

- install or repair water tanks
- install or repair guttering to collect rainwater
- repair taps – for example, replace washers
- build new or better toilets
- organise better rubbish disposal
- make better drains

Parents and citizens could get involved in such a project.

3 Choose a health problem in your school or in the community. Plan some simple activities that can be used to help people to behave in ways that are more healthy. Show your plans to the other students and your teacher. Choose the best ideas and put them into practice.

4 Some schools have become Health Promoting Schools. What do we mean by Health Promoting Schools? Is your school a Health Promoting School? Invite someone to come and talk about Health Promoting Schools.

5 Invite a good role model to come to your school and talk about why he or she does not take harmful drugs. This could be a person who has never taken harmful drugs or someone who took harmful drugs in the past but no longer takes them.

6 Using the words in the list, find the words that are missing from the passage below. You can use each word only once.

| washing | surroundings | adolescence | immunisations | development |
|---|---|---|---|---|
| balanced | adulthood | characteristics | infancy | drugs |
| germs | treat | dangers | | |

We all pass through key stages in our ____________________: from birth, through ____________________ and childhood, into puberty and ____________________, then into ____________________ and old age, and finally death. We all get ____________________ from our parents, but we are also affected by our ____________________ as we grow up. Eating healthy food and a ____________________ diet, taking regular exercise and getting enough rest will help us to grow properly and stay healthy. ____________________ ourselves and our clothes, sheets and towels regularly, and keeping our surroundings clean also help us to stay healthy. Illnesses can be spread by ____________________ and we can prevent sickness by keeping clean, having vaccinations or ____________________ and getting treatment when we are sick. There are ____________________ at school and at home, and we need to learn how to avoid these and stay safe. Drugs or medicines can help to prevent sickness and can be used to ____________________ people who are sick. Some ____________________, like betel nut, tobacco and alcohol, can make people sick.

7 Which of the following best describes the order of events as they occur in our development?
A. adulthood, adolescence, puberty, childhood, birth
B. infancy, adolescence, puberty, adulthood, old age
C. birth, childhood, puberty, adolescence, old age
D. birth, childhood, infancy, puberty, adolescence, adulthood

8 Which of the following help us to grow and develop?
A. Walking to school, working in the garden
B. Eating the same kind of food every day
C. Getting plenty of rest and sleep
D. Feeling unsafe at home and in the community

(a) A, B, and C only
(b) A, C and D only
(c) A, B and D only
(d) A, B, C and D

9 Classify the following characteristics or influences according to whether they come from our parents, the surroundings or our behaviour (some may belong to more than one group).

| Characteristic or influence | Parents | Surroundings | Behaviour |
|---|---|---|---|
| Food – type and amount | | | |
| Height | | | |
| Exercise that we take | | | |
| Insects like mosquitoes that carry malaria | | | |
| Facial features like the size and shape of nose | | | |
| Feeling safe, not being scared or bullied | | | |
| Pollution – breathing dirty or smoky air, drinking or washing in dirty water | | | |
| Colour of skin | | | |
| Personal habits like smoking and drinking | | | |
| Type of hair | | | |
| Keeping clean and hygienic – both your body and the surroundings | | | |
| Shape of body | | | |
| Rest | | | |
| Peer pressure – doing things because your friends do them, or because they 'force' you to do them | | | |

10 List two advantages and two disadvantages of each of the places that you can get information about sexual development in the table below.

| Places that you get information about sexual development | Advantages | Disadvantages |
| --- | --- | --- |
| books | | |
| friends and peers | | |
| teachers | | |
| parents and elders | | |
| newspapers, magazines, radio, television, video | | |

11 In the table below, classify each food according to the group to which it belongs (some may belong to more than one group).

| Food/drink | Energy food | Body-building food (protein) | Protective food |
| --- | --- | --- | --- |
| taro | | | |
| fish | | | |
| coconut milk | | | |
| white rice | | | |
| chicken | | | |
| beans | | | |
| pawpaw | | | |
| sago | | | |
| aibika | | | |
| corned beef | | | |
| mango | | | |
| peanuts | | | |
| corn | | | |
| pork | | | |
| eggs | | | |
| milk | | | |
| margarine | | | |
| tomato | | | |

12 Complete the table by writing the names of different coloured food in each box.

| Colour of food | Energy food | Body-building food (protein) | Protective food |
|---|---|---|---|
| Red foods | | | |
| | | | |
| | | | |
| | | | |
| | | | |
| | | | |
| Yellow foods | | | |
| | | | |
| | | | |
| | | | |
| | | | |
| | | | |

| Colour of food | Energy food | Body-building food (protein) | Protective food |
|---|---|---|---|
| Green foods | | | |
| | | | |
| | | | |
| | | | |
| | | | |
| | | | |
| White foods | | | |
| | | | |
| | | | |
| | | | |
| | | | |
| | | | |

Describe any patterns that you see in the table.

13 The following lists show the food that four people said they ate over several days. Who is most likely to be eating a diet with the best balance of foods from the three food groups?

**Ana** sago, rice, tinned fish, bread, biscuits, noodles, tea, peanuts, coconut milk
**Bau** rice, chicken, aibika, taro, beans, bread, mango, tomato, fish, corn
**Tim** corn, peanuts, aibika, mango, pineapple, beans, sago, cabbage
**Desley** chicken and chips, cake, biscuits, sugar cane, banana, coconut milk

(a) Bau only
(b) Bau and Desley only
(c) Tim, Bau and Ana only
(d) Desley, Tim, Ana and Bau

14 Which of the following best describes the sequence of events when planning, preparing and serving a meal?
A. Keeping cooked food covered before serving.
B. Deciding what type of food to prepare and cook.
C. Looking at the quality of the food before you buy.
D. Keeping hands, utensils and surfaces clean when preparing food.
E. Deciding how much food you are going to cook.

(a) B, E, C, D, A
(b) B, E, C, A, D
(c) D, E, C, B, A
(d) E, B, C, A, D

15 Which of the following are choices and which are not choices about keeping healthy?

| Activity | Choice | No choice |
|---|---|---|
| Bathing every day | | |
| Cutting your foot on broken glass | | |
| Treating sores and keeping them covered | | |
| Eating rubbish foods | | |
| Keeping my nose clean | | |
| Catching 'red eye' in the dry season | | |
| Chewing betel nut with lime | | |
| Combing and washing hair regularly | | |
| Getting diarrhoea even though you wash your hands before touching food | | |
| Smoking cigarettes | | |

16 Match the common illnesses with the way that they are spread. (Two of the illnesses can be spread in the same way.)

| Illness | How is the problem caused? |
|---|---|
| tinea or ringworm | caused by a mite that lives on the skin |
| malaria | caused by bacteria and affects the lungs – spread by coughing |
| dengue | carried by mosquitoes that bite in the daytime |
| tuberculosis | spread by food and drink |
| typhoid (affects the digestive system) | fungus that grows on the skin |
| scabies | carried by mosquitoes that bite at night |
| gastroenteritis (diarrhoea) | |

**Questions 17–19 refer to the following list of ways that you can protect yourself from illness.**

A. Wash and keep hands clean – especially after going to the toilet and before touching food.
B. Wash eating and cooking utensils with hot water.
C. Keep the home and the surroundings clean. Remove places where mosquitoes can lay eggs in water.
D. Sleep under mosquito nets.
E. Cover your mouth when coughing and sneezing.
F. Wash clothes, towels and bed sheets regularly and dry in the sun.
G. Always follow instructions when taking medicine – especially when taking antibiotics or medicine for malaria.
H. Cooked food should be eaten when it is hot. Do not eat cooked food that has been kept warm for many hours. Keep food covered.
I. Have only safe sexual contact.

17 Which of the following are ways to protect yourself from diarrhoea?
(a) A only
(b) A and B
(c) A, B and H
(d) A, B, G and H

18 Which of the following are ways to protect yourself against malaria?
(a) A and C
(b) C and D
(c) C, D and G
(d) C, D, E and G

19 Which activities require a regular water supply in order to be able to carry them out every day?
(a) A only
(b) A and B
(c) A, B and C
(d) A, B and F

20 A risk is something that you do that can have a bad effect on your health or well-being. A hazard is a danger that we find in our surroundings. Classify the following according to whether each is a risk or a hazard.

| | Risk | Hazard |
|---|---|---|
| Wells containing animal faeces | | |
| No proper toilets so people use the bush | | |
| Rubbish spread all over the village | | |
| Too many people sleeping close together in the same house | | |
| Not enough windows or shutters to let in fresh air | | |
| Sea urchins and stonefish | | |
| Using a canoe when there are strong winds | | |
| Sitting under a coconut tree | | |
| Playing with fire | | |
| People fighting | | |
| People getting drunk | | |

21 Which of the following describes the causes of health problems and the ways that health problems are spread in the community?

A. Germs like bacteria and viruses
B. Insects and rats that can carry germs
C. The surroundings that have dirty water or dirty air
D. People's behaviour

(a) A and B
(b) B and C
(c) A, B and C
(d) A, B, C and D

22 Which of the following drugs are controlled by national laws in Papua New Guinea?
A. Alcohol like beer, wine and spirits
B. Tea and coffee which both contain caffeine
C. Tobacco including brus and cigarettes
D. Betel nut and lime

23 Which of the following best describes prescription drugs?
A. A chemical substance that changes the body in some way
B. Drugs that a doctor decides to give to you
C. Drugs that both prevent and cure sickness
D. Drugs that do not have unpleasant side-effects

24 Which of the following are health reasons for taking drugs and which are non-health reasons?

| | Health reasons | Non-health reasons |
|---|---|---|
| To celebrate and feel relaxed | | |
| To try to forget problems | | |
| To prevent an illness | | |
| Because other people are doing it | | |
| To cure a disease | | |
| Because parents or friends try to persuade | | |
| Because it is something that adults do | | |
| To find out what it feels like | | |
| To avoid feeling sad | | |

25 Do you agree or disagree with the following statements about HIV/AIDS? Give reasons for your choices.

(a) If you catch a sexually transmitted infection like HIV it is usually because of the way that you behave.

(b) If you do not have sex before you get married and then husband and wife only have sex with each other, then they will not catch a sexually transmitted infection like HIV.

(c) Any person who has sexual intercourse with more than one person is at risk of catching a sexually transmitted infection including HIV.

(d) You can usually tell if a person has a sexually transmitted infection like HIV just by looking at them.

(e) If you think that you may have caught a sexually transmitted infection like HIV then you should go and see a health worker as soon as possible.

# Chapter 5: Living and working together

1 Invite a councillor or other respected person from the community to come and talk about the value of different rules and laws.

2 Invite a policeman or policewoman to come and talk about their work in the community.

3 If your school is near a town, find out when the District Court or National Court is sitting and arrange a visit to the court. Or invite a magistrate to visit your school and talk about the work of the courts.

4 Use a questionnaire like the one below to carry out a survey about the attitudes of students in your school and people in the local community. Some questions have been included, but you can write more of your own.

| Question | Strongly agree | Agree | Disagree | Strongly disagree |
|---|---|---|---|---|
| People who break the law should be punished | | | | |
| Everyone is free to do as they please | | | | |
| People should feel safe everywhere they go | | | | |
| Girls do not have the same freedom as boys | | | | |
| Rules should be different for boys and girls | | | | |
| The biggest problem in the community is people breaking the law | | | | |

5 Using the words in the list, find the words that are missing from the passage below. You can use each word only once.

| | | | | |
|---|---|---|---|---|
| behaviour | community | leader | freedoms | useful |
| influences | rights | qualities | laws | decisions |

People have different ____________________. These qualities can help them to be a good and ____________________ member of a group. Not everybody can be a leader, and to be a good and fair ____________________ the person must have certain qualities. Everybody must follow the rules and laws of the ____________________. These rules and laws guide our ____________________. Rules and ____________________ help to protect us and keep us safe. All people also have ____________________ and freedoms, and we must also respect the rights and ____________________ of other people. Everybody can make good ____________________ in their life by following certain steps. There are different ____________________ on the way that we make decisions.

6 In the right hand column, write down words that are the opposite of the positive qualities of a group member shown in the left hand column.

| Positive quality of a group member | Negative quality of a group member |
|---|---|
| Fair | |
| Loyal or faithful | |
| Helpful | |
| Hard working | |
| Kind | |
| Caring | |
| Trustworthy | |
| Honest | |
| Reliable | |

7 Which of the following best describes the sequence or order of the steps that you go through in making a decision about something important in your life?

A. Ask: 'What are the options and choices that I can make?'
B. Think about all the possibilities and make your decision.
C. Ask: 'What is the issue or the problem?'
D. Ask: 'What are the good things and bad things that can happen as a result of each option?'

(a) C, A, B, D
(b) C, A, D, B
(c) A, C, D, B
(d) D, C, A, B

8 Which of the following are all qualities of a good and fair leader?

A. Honest and can be trusted
B. Can solve problems peacefully
C. Knows and understands people in the community
D. Interested in helping himself before he helps others

(a) A and B only
(b) A and C only
(c) A, B and C only
(d) A, B, C and D

9 Which of the following statements are true and which are false?

| Statement | True or false? |
|---|---|
| All rules and laws show people the way that they should behave. | |
| Some rules may be different in different places. | |
| Some people are allowed to break the laws of the country. | |
| Rewards encourage people to follow rules and laws. | |
| Punishment always stops people breaking rules and laws. | |

# The Community Game

## Everyone's a winner!

### To play the game you will need

One dice (you can make your own if you do not have one)
One different marker for each player

## How to play

The first player throws the dice. The number on the dice is the number of squares that the player moves.
Each player then takes a turn.
If you land on a square with writing you must follow the instruction.
The winners are the ones who find themselves in a safe and healthy home.

# Glossary

**achievement** an activity which has been completed successfully.

**addiction** being dependent on taking drugs.

**adolescence** the period between puberty and maturity when children change into adults.

**antibiotics** a kind of medicine that is made from microbes and used to cure a person who has a sickness caused by bacteria or fungi.

**attack** trying to score points or goals against another team in a game of sport.

**bacteria** small living organisms that are found in the air, in water, on food and in the ground. Some bacteria can make people sick, but sicknesses caused by bacteria can usually be cured with antibiotics. See **antibiotics**.

**carbohydrate** a type of food such as sugar and starch which provides energy in the diet.

**characteristics** qualities that are typical of a person or some other living thing or object.

**coach** someone who teaches or trains others, for example, in sport.

**Cooperative Society** business owned and controlled by local people in Papua New Guinea.

**coordination** to make different things happen at the same time.

**defend** trying to prevent the other team scoring points or goals in a game of sport.

**dehydration** not enough water in the body. This may be caused by sweating, vomiting or diarrhoea. The dehydrated person may not have much energy, but they do not always feel thirsty and young children can die when they are dehydrated. The treatment is to drink plenty of water with a little sugar added, but in some cases a health worker may need to put a drip in the person's arm.

**dengue** also called breakbone fever. A sickness caused by a virus and carried by some mosquitoes that bite in the daytime. It causes a fever and pain in the bones.

**development** the changes that take place in people as they grow from children into adults.

**didiman** a person who works for the government and helps people to learn how to grow better crops or look after different kinds of animals.

**diet 1** the mixture of foods that people eat. It is important to eat the right amount of food from the three food groups, which are growth foods such as protein, energy foods such as carbohydrates, and protective foods such as fresh fruit and vegetables. This is called a balanced diet. **2** to control the type and amount of food that you eat.

**digestive system** the system of the body that breaks down food, beginning with the mouth and ending with the anus.

**draw** a way of deciding which teams will play each other in a sports competition.

**dribble** to carefully move the ball forward little by little in a game of soccer or basketball.

**environment** the surroundings which may influence our growth, development and behaviour.

**extended family** a family consisting of children, their parents, grandparents and possibly uncles and aunts living closely together.

**fat** one of three types of food that are needed in the diet.

**food poisoning** an illness that affects the digestive system. Food poisoning is usually caused by eating food containing bacteria or poisonous chemicals.

**gastroenteritis** a sickness of the stomach and intestines. It is usually due to infection by viruses or bacteria or to food poisoning. It causes vomiting and diarrhoea.

**gender** being a girl or a boy, a man or a woman, which we learn from the community.

**germs** small living things that can make us sick.

**grille** a skin disease caused by a fungus that grows on the skin, often forming a pattern of circles or rings; also known as ringworm, tinea and sipoma.

**hazard** a danger that is found in our surroundings.

**identity** individuality or personality.

**immunisation** a way of preventing sickness by giving a person an injection. Most immunisations are given to children, so parents must take their children to the clinic to get them immunised. Immunisations are recorded in a little book which the parents should keep in a safe place so that they know which sicknesses their children are protected against. See **vaccination**.

**infant** a child under one year of age. A child that cannot live without its mother.

**inherited** obtained from our parents.

**injection** forcing drugs or some other liquid into a part of the body by using a syringe.

**kiap** a patrol officer who carried out the work of the government in Papua New Guinea.

**leisure** free time.

**line umpire** someone who helps the referee or umpire to decide if the ball has crossed the line in a game of sport.

**long jump pit** a hole in the ground that is filled with sand and used for the long jump and the high jump.

**luluai** a village elder or 'big man' in Papua New Guinea who was chosen to help carry out the work of the government in his village. See **tultul**.

**malaria** a disease caused by a germ called a protozoan which lives in the blood and is carried by some mosquitoes. People with malaria often have shivering, fever and sweating which can happen again and again; in some cases people can die. Malaria can be prevented by not being bitten or by taking chloroquine; it can also be treated with chloroquine or other drugs. There is more malaria on the coast than in the highlands of Papua New Guinea.

**malnutrition** not eating the amount and type of food that is needed to be healthy. This is very important when children are still growing.

**microbe** any living thing that is too small to be seen with the naked eye; for example bacteria, viruses and some fungi and protozoa.

**mite** a little animal that lives in the skin and causes itching.

**nickname** a name added to, or used in place of, a person's real name.

**nourishing** food that is healthy and satisfying.

**nuclear family** a family consisting of children and their parents living together.

**nutrition** **1** the study of food. **2** the food that people eat and the way that their bodies use that food.

**penicillin** an antibiotic that is made from a mould or fungus.

**period** when a girl or woman has a period, a small amount of blood and mucus flows from the uterus out of the vagina. Periods start when a girl is about 13 and continue about once a month until the age of 45 – 55, when they stop. This is a perfectly natural thing to happen, and a woman having her period is not dirty and can do normal things. When a girl starts to have her periods it means that she can have a baby, and when she is pregnant her periods stop; missing a period is often the first sign that a woman is pregnant.

**pharmacist** a person who works in an pharmacy and is allowed to give drugs to patients who have a prescription from a doctor.

**prescription** a written instruction from a doctor to a pharmacist for preparing and providing drugs for a patient.

**protein** a type of food in the diet that, after being digested, is used in growth to form muscles, tissues and organs.

**puberty** the period of sexual development.

**recreation** things that we do to relax and enjoy ourselves. See **leisure**.

**responsibility** **1** being trustworthy and able to answer for the way that you behave. **2** the job that a person has to do.

**risk** a behaviour that can have a bad effect on our health or well-being.

**role** the part that a person plays in a family, at school, in a sports team etc.

**scabies** a disease caused by a little animal called a mite that burrows into the skin, causing bad itching.

**sculling** gently moving the hands and arms to stay afloat in the water or move a little. See **treading water**.

**semen** the creamy liquid that comes out of the penis during sexual intercourse and that contains sperm.

**sex** being a male or a female. Also means sexual contact between a man and a woman.

**sexual development** the changes that take place in our bodies as we develop from a girl to a woman and a boy into a man. See also **puberty**.

**sexuality** the way that we think, feel and behave because we are a male or a female.

**sexually transmitted infection (STI)** also called sexually transmitted disease or venereal disease. Most STIs are caused by bacteria and many (though not all) can be cured by antibiotics if the person gets treatment early enough. AIDS, donovanosis, gonorrhoea and syphilis are all STIs.

**shoot** to aim for the goal in a game of sport, for example, netball, soccer.

**sign** something that a health worker notices that shows that a person is sick, but which the person does not notice.

**sperm** the male sex cell. Sperm are usually found in semen and a single sperm fertilises the egg at the time of conception.

**spleen** an organ on the left hand side of the body, below and behind the stomach.

**sports injury** any injury which occurs as a result of playing sport. Sports injuries often affect muscles, ligaments and tendons.

**symptoms** something that a person notices which shows that the person is sick.

**timekeeper** a person who records the time taken, for example, during a game of sport.

**treading water** gently moving the legs and arms to stay afloat in the water. See **sculling.**

**tuberculosis (TB)** a disease caused by bacteria which usually affects the lungs and can cause people to have fever, spit blood and lose weight. People with TB can spread germs when they cough.

**tultul** a village elder or 'big man' in Papua New Guinea who was chosen to help carry out the work of the government in his village. See **luluai.**

**typhoid** a disease caused by bacteria that affects the intestines. It causes general weakness, red spots on the skin, chills and sweating. It is transmitted through food or drinking water that is contaminated with faeces or urine from an infected person. People usually recover naturally but the disease can be treated with antibiotics.

**vaccination** a way of protecting a person against a disease. A vaccine is usually given by injection, but can also be given by mouth or scratching the skin. See **immunisation**.

**values** the things that people say or think are important.

**virus** a very small microbe that lives on other organisms and so makes them sick. The common cold, influenza, measles, mumps, chickenpox and AIDS are caused by viruses. Many diseases caused by viruses can be controlled by vaccines, and drugs can be used to treat others.

# Some Common Diseases

| Disease | Common symptoms |
|---|---|
| **Chicken pox** | **Symptoms may include:**<br>• a rash<br>• an itchy feeling<br>• a runny nose<br>• a rash that looks like red spots which usually starts on the chest, back and face |
| **Diarrhoea** | **Symptoms may include:**<br>• stools or bowel movements which are loose or watery and which may contain blood, pus or fat droplets<br>• abdominal pain<br>• nausea<br>• vomiting<br>• general weakness |
| **Dengue fever** | **Symptoms may include:**<br>fever, rash as well as severe pain in bones, joints and muscles |
| **Gastroenteritis** | **Symptoms may include:**<br>loss of appetite, vomiting, cramps, nausea, diarrhoea |
| **Gonorrhoea** | **Symptoms may include:**<br>• a burning sensation when urinating<br>• frequent urination<br>• pus-like discharge from the vagina or penis<br>• tenderness or pain in the genital area or abdomen<br>• for women, bleeding between menstrual cycles |
| **German measles** | **Symptoms may include:**<br>a rash on the face, a slight fever and sometimes the lymph nodes at the back of the neck become swollen |
| **Infectious hepatitis** | **Symptoms may include:**<br>• exhaustion<br>• loss of appetite<br>• nausea, darkening of urine<br>• abdominal pain<br>• yellowish tinging of the skin and the whites of the eyes |
| **Influenza (flu)** | **Symptoms may include:**<br>• high fever<br>• chilled feeling<br>• sore throat<br>• aching of the whole body<br>• coughing and sneezing<br>• chest congestion |

| Disease | Common symptoms | |
|---|---|---|
| Malaria | **Symptoms may include:**<br>chills, fever, sweating, headache, aching muscles, tiredness, vomiting, diarrhoea, coughing | |
| Pneumonia | **Symptoms may include:**<br>• fever • chills that cause the body to shake<br>• quick and crackly breathing • bad headache<br>• loss of appetite, tiredness • nausea • vomiting<br>• coughing which may result in large amounts of thick, greenish mucus being brought up | |
| Syphilis | **Symptoms may include:**<br>• sores on the body, particularly in the area of the genitals • loss of patches of hair<br>• a rash which is usually on the palms of the hands and the soles of the feet<br>• aching body • tiredness • fever | |
| Tuberculosis | The symptoms depend on where in the body the tuberculosis bacteria are growing | |
| | **The lungs** | Symptoms may include:<br>• cough that won't go away • chest pain<br>• coughing up blood or sputum • lack of appetite<br>• fever • chills and sweating at night |
| | **The urinary tract** | Symptoms may include:<br>• repeated urinary tract infections • repeated fevers<br>• pus or blood in the urine |
| | **The brain** | Symptoms may include: headaches, seizures and abnormal behaviour |
| | **The lymph nodes** | Symptoms may include: inflammation and swelling on nodes anywhere in the body including in the neck |
| | **Bones and joints** | Symptoms may include: fever, pain as well as stiff and swollen joints |
| | **Peritoneum** | Symptoms may include: fever and a build-up of fluid inside the abdomen |
| | **Heart** (rare) | Symptoms may include: shortness of breath, chest pain and fever. |

*Source: Izenberg Neil M.D. (editor in chief), *Human Diseases and Conditions*, Volumes 1, 2 and 3, Charles Scribner's Sons, New York, 2000

**Other Diseases**

Amoebic dysentery
Athletes foot
Cholera
Diphtheria
German measles
Tinea versicolor (white spot)
Impetigo
Measles
Mumps
Poliomyelitis (polio)
Ringworm
Smallpox
Tetanus
Typhoid
Whooping cough
Ascariasis
Bacillary dysentery
Common cold
Filariasis (elephantiasis)
Tinea imbricarta (grille)
Hookworm
Leprosy
Plague
Rabies
Scabies
Tapeworm
Threadworm
Typhus
Yaws

A person with AIDS is just like You and Me
That's because AIDS can happen to anyone. It doesn't discriminate by age, gender, cultural background, social status or religion. We should all provide care and support for people living with the AIDS virus to ensure that they can continue to live productively for many years to come.
For Further Information about AIDS in your Community contact:
Protect yourself from
AIDS
Supported by the Australian Government
PNG National AIDS Council
Don't have sex, be faithful or always use a condom